THE GREAT AWAKENING

Volume XV

Temple Teachings from the
Higher Realms

Sister Thedra

Copyright © 2021 by Halls of Light, LLC

All rights reserved. This book or any portion thereof may not be reproduced or used in any manner whatsoever without the express written permission of the publisher except for the use of brief quotations in a book review.

ISBN: 978-1-7366487-0-4

To the Reader

This book is only a portion of the teachings and prophecies that have been given by Sananda, Sanat Kumara, and others of the higher realms, and Recorded by Sister Thedra.

Contents

MEDITATION 1

TRANSMUTATION 67

UPON MY HOLY MT 97

BY THEIR FRUIT... 145

SACRED SYMBOLS 201

Mission Statement 234

Sananda's Appearance 235

Authority to Use the Name Sananda 236

About the Late Sister Thedra 238

Esu Jesus Sananda

This reproduction is from an actual photograph taken on June 1st, 1961, in Chichen Itza, Yucatan, by one of thirty archaeologists working in the area at the time. Sananda appeared in visible, tangible body and permitted His photograph to be taken.

MEDITATION

Soar with me - into infinite space - wherein is no matter - no thing - bring with thee nothing ----

Come with me -- call from the source of thy being thy own LIGHT.

Bring not thy fortune of earth -- thy leg irons --

Leave that which is of earth behind -- dwell with me this moment within the GODHOOD -- wherein there are no bounds --

Wherein there is only LIGHT -- Freedom from all care - all woe.

Fear not for I AM with thee -- and I shall bear thee out - and I shall be unto thee all THE FATHER would have me be - So be it and Selah.

Blest are they which walk with me -- and they shall know me for that which I am - and I AM He which was - and which is - and ever shall be - So be it and SELAH.

Blest AM I - and blest shall ye be --

I AM HE which has given unto thee expression --

I AM HE which was before ABRAHAM was --

I AM HE which was before thy galaxy came into being --

I AM HE which has been called by many names - yet I AM NAMELESS --

I AM ----

And I shall call myself AUM SOLEN - for a purpose which shall be unto thee thy "SHIELD and THY BUCKLER" --

I SHALL BE UNTO THEE ALL THINGS --

I shall give unto thee thy inheritance which is thy GODHOOD ---

Meditate upon thy OWN SOURCE -- and give unto thyself credit for being MY SON - MY DAUGHTER ---

And I say unto thee: YE SHALL BE GLAD FOREVER MORE -- So be it and SELAH -

Sanat Kumara speaking -

Beloved ones which gather thyself together, which are together as one assembly - I say ye shall be as "one" for there is none other than the Mighty I AM - I say unto thee: ye are the One and the expression of the One Almighty I AM - I say ye are because of the I AM which is, was - and ever shall be -

I say ye are fortuned to be because ye are one with the presence which never dies and which is not born -

I say ye are that which was from the beginning and which shall endure unto the end -

I say that ye are because there is a part of the Mighty Presence which has gone out as a feeling - thinking entity - which ye think thyself to be Ye know not that which ye are - Ye have had thy memory blanked from thee and ye have forgotten thy being -

Ye are as the wayward son - Ye shall now return unto thy rightful ESTATE - Ye shall return this day unto thy Father-Mother God from whence ye went out as a thing apart - yet one with them -

Ye shall know this day thy oneness with them and ye shall be as one which has a crown upon thy head and ye shall walk which way it tilts not - Blest are they which walk upright -

Be ye as one blest of me and by me and I shall lift thee up as the Condor lifts up the lamb - So be it and Selah -

Be ye as one prepared for that which I shall give unto thee at sunrise. I have waited for this time -

I am and I know myself to be - So be it and Selah -

Sanat Kumara -

Sister Thedra of the Emerald Cross

Sanat Kumara speaking -

Ye have come unto this altar for the purpose of learning of the greater law - Now hear me in this - And be ye mindful of these my words - for I say again that there are none so sad as the ones which betray themself -

Now it is given unto me to know whereof I speak and ye shall give unto me credit for knowing the law - And I say unto thee: ye are as one bound by thy pore and ye see not beyond thy own limitation - I say thy <u>own</u> limitation - None other limits thee -

Ye have <u>as yet</u> not accepted thy inheritance which the Father has willed unto thee -

Ye have as yet not become wise - I say ye shall in due time learn the law which governs all things - Yet for this shall ye be prepared -

I say when ye are so prepared one shall come unto thee and give unto thee such as shall be unto thee all that is necessary unto thy learning - Ye shall know and know that ye know -

This is revelation and I say that in this day which is come this new age which is now here within thy realm all things shall be revealed - unto the ones which are prepared for such knowledge -

I say ye which prepare thyself shall have these laws revealed unto thee -

Yet ye shall be at all times true unto thyself -

And ye shall be worthy of such as this entails - I say great is the responsibility of one which holds the key to the Kingdom -

And blest is he which is found worthy - I am not so foolish as to give unto babes at the breast my pearls which know not their worth -

I am prepared for this day and I say none pilfer my pockets - and call me foolish - I am about my Father's business and I am now prepared to come unto them which are prepared to receive - And I shall give unto them that which is wise and prudent - And I say glad shall they be for their preparation - Now let it again go on record that thy tongue is thy pitfall wherein ye trip -

Be ye as one mindful of every word which proceeds out of thy mouth -

And I say unto thee - Ye are as ones which have upon thy own shoulders the responsibility of that which ye send forth upon the eth - either in jest or in all sincerity of purpose -

I say the law knows no favorite - It produces after its kind - and the spoken word shall produce either peace, or there shall be a portion which ye shall find very bitter -

Blest is he which uses this law for the good of his own soul -

Amen and Selah -

I am with thee and so shall ye be blest of me and by me - Give not that which is for thee unto them which would misuse it -

Be ye blest this day -

I am thy brother and thy Sibor -

Sanat Kumara

Sister Thedra of the Emerald Cross

Sanat Kumara speaking -

Beloved of my being - be ye blest of my presence for I am with thee. Blest are they which come into my presence for they shall be blest as I have been blest -

I am now prepared to give unto thee as I have received - And ye shall be as one lifted up - And ye shall be freed from all bondage forever. So be it and Selah -

Now say unto them which come into thy presence that they shall prepare themself for a part which shall be new unto them and they shall be as ones alert for they shall be as ones on whose shoulders rest the responsibility of their own salvation -

I say they shall prepare themself and I say - The law has been given unto them and it is plainly and simply written - And none shall say it is not so - I declare unto them I have plainly given unto them the law - so simply stated that they may overlook it -

Be ye not misled by great and grand sounding frases (phrases) for they mean NOTHING according to thy salvation - And take into account thy own welfare - What profit thee if you receive of man great applauds and are cast out of thy Father's house?

Pity are they which betray themself - I say the words of God the Father shall be put into the mouth of lowly and the just -

Children shall speak words of wisdom while the learned - and the worldly wise - them which <u>think</u> themself wise shall be as the foolish which have thrown overboard their life belts - Pity shall they be -- I say pity are they for they betray themself -

I am glad for the just and the ones which have surrendered up their little will unto the Father that His will might be done in them - through them - and by them These shall He glorify - Amen and Selah -

Might is His power and great His glory - Praise His Holy Name -

So great shall be thy joy thy heart shall open wide that ye may receive of Him thy orb and thy scepter -

I am thy brother - Sanat Kumara -

Sister Thedra of the Emerald Cross

Sananda speaking -

Blest are they which come unto this altar which the Father has caused to be brought into manifestation - I say they shall be blest - So be it and Selah -

Sanat Kumara has spoken unto thee of the law and he has done well.

I say ye have not seen - Nor have ye heard that which he has said -

He has given unto thee the Keys unto the Kingdom and ye have given it little thought - Ye have not turned the key in the gate -

Nor have ye given unto thyself the discipline which is necessary for a disciple of the Christ - Ye have as yet not walked in the way set before thee - Ye have gone out from thy places of abode as one of them - Ye have spoken as they speak - Ye have dressed as they dress - Ye have followed them in their way - Ye have been unto them one of them

Ye have not spoken of thy own word* Ye have said that which they would have thee say - Ye have given of thy time unto frivolity - Ye have said that which is not prompted by love - Ye have gone the long way to say that which ye think -

Ye have not been a shining example of a disciple of the Christ - Which is thy own light which never fails -

Ye have gone to and fro as ones sent forth to battle - With thy cross upon thy back - Ye have not as yet found Peace - Ye have as yet not found that which ye seek -

Ye have gone the long way that ye may not have to account for thy actions - for thy misused energy -

Now hear me in this - Each and every one shall cleanse his own altar and he shall find therein many things which shall profit him to transmute - And he shall be his own Alchemist -

He shall come unto this altar clean of heart and clean of hands - He shall be of himself the judge - He shall have none other -

Yet the law is a cold and calculating thing - It plays no favorites - He which tries to deceive himself is a traitor indeed - And the greatest of fools -

Blest are they which are true unto themself and come of their own free will - and bring themself as a living sacrifice - for none other can we use -

Blest be this day - Blest shall ye be - Amen and Selah -

I am thy Sibor and thy brother - Sananda -

* Deceit

Sister Thedra of the Emerald Cross

Beloved of my being - Ye shall now receive of the beloved brother which we know as Soran and he has come unto this temple as one prepared for that which he is to do - Ye shall be glad when ye find him waiting for thee wherein ye shall be brought -

I say ye shall now be prepared to be brought to the place wherein we are and ye shall be glad for thy preparation - for herein ye shall find that which ye have written from thy own hand - Ye shall find that which ye have written by thy own hand laying upon the altar of white alabaster wherein stands thy older brother -

Sanat Kumara now stands as the Comanche - or the Most Worthy Grand Master - which shall declare for thee thy freedom forever -

Beloved: Ye shall give unto them this word - that there is a great and grand council which now sits in session for the purpose of freeing them which have chosen to go the ROYAL ROAD -

I say we are assembled together in JOY and THANKSGIVING that these our brothers have come unto this altar for the purpose of being prepared for their ascension - And I say one has gone out from us as one eternally free -

And I say ye have been blest - to have upon thy film the part which shall bear witness of that which has been recorded - So be it that proof shall go into the records with the written word - So be it and Selah -

Now I say ye shall again find it the better part of wisdom to be alert and watchful - for there shall be a great demonstration of our force which has been gathered within this temple which has been dedicated unto truth and justice for so many ages past -

I am glad ye shall be brought in - Amen - So be it -

I am thy brother Soran -

Sister Thedra of the Emerald Cross

Soran speaking -

Ye have yet to be as one brought into the place wherein I am - For this do ye wait - Too I say ye shall be as one which shall stand before this altar of white alabaster whereupon ye shall find the symbol which has been given unto thee and which is engraved upon thy heart -

For I say ye have in time passed stood upon the altar of alabaster - whereupon ye left thy own name - and whereupon ye shall find the record written in imperishable gold leaves - A tablet of gold - Not touched with hand - It is taken from the eth and it shall remain intact for all ages to come -

Now be ye as one prepared for ye shall come into this place for a time and ye shall return unto them - and ye shall give unto them as ye have received - So be it and Selah -

Be ye as one on whose shoulders rest great responsibility - And ye shall remember that which has been given unto thee to do and ye shall be as one prepared for greater things -

Give unto none the power to take from thee - Nor to give unto thee.

Be ye one which can keep thy own council - and ask of no man his opinion -

Bless them in their unknowing - And yet ye shall not be part of their frivolity - their foolishness -

Ye shall remember thy responsibility at all times -

Ye shall measure not thy ability unto anothers -

Ye shall not put thyself into the place of another -

Ye shall be as one which has thy place - thy part - and be glad for thy part - Rejoice in all things and remember them which sibor thee - And bless them and receive them joyously - and a host shall administer unto thy need -

I am thy Sibor and thy older brother - Soran -

Sister Thedra of the Emerald Cross

Bor speaking -

Be ye blest of my presence and of my being - For I come that ye may be blest - Accept my blessing in the name of the Father which has given unto us being -

By my hand shall ye be blest - I say ye shall be blest by my hand for I am not a far off - I am near unto thee - And I know thee even as I know myself - For I know myself as I AM -

I fear naught - Therefore I shall speak fearlessly - For none shall stay me nor shall they persecute my hand made manifest -

I say my handmaiden shall not be persecuted for my share - Nor shall she be spat upon -

Blest are my servants for they shall dwell in the House of the Lord.-

Blest is the House of the Lord - for therein dwells the ones which have gone the Royal Road - And I say unto them which have chosen this path of initiation - them which do endure unto the end - that it is not an easy path - Yet it is the day of initiation and a new dispensation is given unto thee - Ye have but to prepare thyself to receive that which is willed unto thee from the beginning -

I say it is the simple way - It is given unto me to know all the ways.

There are long and tortuous routes - but the one set before thee is the simple one - Which the Lord and Master Jesus - Sananda - <u>Thy Master</u> set before thee so long ago -

Ye are now prepared to face the day of great decision which shall be thy own to make - for none other shall make it for thee -

Keep thy own council - for it is the better part of wisdom - Even thy friends know not that which lies ahead of thee - For ye have been through this before -

I say ye have trod these paths before - Even as I have - I say I too have walked upon the shores of the great seas -

I have looked upon the lakes from the mountain tops - I have walked the shores with sandaled feet - I have been as man - And I too have gone the Royal Road - From the high Andes did I make my ascension so long ago - Ye have no account of it -

Ye know me not for I am one of the ones which have worked in silence that this day may bear fruit -

I come unto this, my hand maiden for the reason she called me brother in the early days of thy homeland - She used to bring unto me the cup of liquid from the poatal wherein stood a jar of pure wine not made by hand - which was precipitated from the ether -

I say unto thee - Ye shall come to know many things which thy history has not recorded - for the greatest of all records are not available unto the uninitiated - So shall they* be just in all their ways ere they shall become available -

I am in the place wherein I am prepared to reveal many things unto them which are prepared to receive it - that which shall be wise and prudent -

Blest shall they be -

I am Bor -

Sister Thedra of the Emerald Cross

* The candidate.

Sarah - Mother of Abraham speaking -

I say unto thee my children - I have given of myself that ye may have thy being in me and of me - I say I have given unto thee expression I have brought thee into being - And I have caused thee to Be - I AM therefore thou art -

Beside thee there is none other - for I AM and ye are me - I AM thee and I say ye are not separated from me - only in thy UN-Knowing. Now it is come when ye shall know - and KNOW that ye KNOW - And for this have ye waited -

Long have ye waited in darkness - Long have ye wandered in the valleys of despair - Long have ye looked for peace - wherein ye have found naught except longing and suffering -

Now I say ye shall turn thy face homeward - And I shall touch thee and I shall awaken thee and ye shall wonder at thy sleep -

I say unto thee AWAKEN!

Oh, my children - I await thee - Alert thyself and return unto me and I shall receive thee unto myself as my own as though thou hast not wandered afar from me - Bring thy heart - thy hand and thy will and I shall make of thee that which ye have waited to become -

I say ye shall become a Son of God - even as ye went out -

Ye shall return unto me even as ye went out - Blest are they which return this day - And I shall await thy return with great joy -

Be ye blest of me and by me - So be it and Selah -

I am thy Mother Sarah -

* * * * * * * *

Soran speaking -

Be ye blest of me and by my presence - I come after our Blessed Parent God - which has given unto us being -

Ye which are the hand made manifest shall be as one qualified to speak for Her - for She shall put her words into thy mouth and ye shall know that which ye say and ye shall be glad for this day - I come from out the place wherein She - our Mother abides -

Blest are they which are fortunate to know Her and by Her love and mercy shall She bring thee home - I AM - because SHE IS - and I am glad - I am - Soran

Sister Thedra of the Emerald Cross

Portions of the Sibors

The Greater Truths Cannot be written

Sarah - Mother of Abraham speaking: -

Blest art thou O my child - blest are they which come into the place wherein I am and I shall be unto them that which shall sustain them ---

I say I shall sustain them - I shall be unto them all that they need be. They shall know me to be - and they shall know themself to be - and they shall know themself to be one with me - and they shall separate themself from me no more ---

For they shall be even as I - they shall be as ones come alive - and they shall know no more death - for I say they shall not die ---

Now it is come when they which choose to follow within this - the way set before thee - shall have the choice of going within the secret places of Earth - wherein they may serve the children which are yet in bondage - or they may return unto their abiding place from which they went out -- I say they shall be free to choose the place wherein they shall serve ---

Now remember that which ye have forgotten and be unto thyself true - and ask for Light from the Source of all Light - from which all knowledge cometh - and be ye not misled -- Ye findeth not such knowledge within the books of thy libraries - ye find it not within thy temples made with hands - For the TRUTH which IS- HAS BEEN and NEVER SHALL CHANGE - cannot be contained within pages of all thy books - nor can it be spoken ---

I say unto thee O my children - ye are on the verge of great discoveries ---

Ye have waited long and impatient have ye been -- Now ye shall learn to love one another and ye shall be unto each other comfort - ye shall be unto the other an example of the Living Christ ---

Ye shall bless thyself and ye shall walk upright and deal justly in all thy ways -- Ye shall be unto all which enter into thy dwelling place an example of the initiate - ye shall bless them and give unto them of thy own self ---

Let no man put false words into thy mouth - repeat naught which would besmirch another -- Remember thy Golden Rule and live as tho ye had it within thy heart - and come unto the altar with clean hands and mind ---

Cleanse thy mind - purify thy thots as ye would thy hands - they can and do contaminate thee -- Cleanse thy heart of all thy own smallness - and be ye as one which has my hand upon thee at all times and I shall bless thee and bring thee home ---

So be it ye shall be victorious in the end -- I have spoken - ye have heard me -- Blest be this day ---

I am thy Mother

Sister Thedra of the Emerald Cross

A Master of the Elements

Sananda speaking: -

Sarah - Mother of Abraham has given unto me this part for thee that they may have it -- Now let it be recorded that they may know that which is said unto thee and for this have ye waited

Now it has been recorded many times that there shall be a great awakening - and it is truly so - and it is now come when one shall walk among thee as one of them which has come into the Earth as flesh made manifest and as one of Earth ---

Yet I say unto thee - he shall be as thou art - yet he shall have a body of light substance - and it shall not bind him - he shall be master of it - he shall be free to go and come at will -- He shall be able to take with him his body and he shall be master of the elements -- So be it and Selah ---

Be it so that this one shall walk among thee and ye shall be alert and watchful - for he shall be in the place wherein I am for a time - then he shall go out as one prepared for a new part - and he shall be in the place wherein ye are for a part which shall be revealed unto thee ---

Ye shall walk which way he shall approve -- Ye shall be unto thyself true - for he shall not be deceived - he shall know thee as ye are and he shall be unto his trust true ---

He shall give unto the just and the prudent as they are prepared to receive - they shall bring unto the altar that which is their harvest -- They shall bring unto the altar that which they are - and they shall be as ones on whose shoulders rests their own salvation ---

They shall be known by their fruit - they shall be as ones which has the crown upon their head - for they shall be crowned by the Father-Mother God ---

They shall be as ones lifted up - they shall be as ones freed from all bondage forever - they shall be as ones hailed forever as Sons of God.

Praises shall ring out from every mountain top: HAIL - HE IS RISEN - HE HAS RECEIVED HIS FREEDOM - IT IS COME WHEN HE HAS RETURNED! HE HAS RETURNED - HE IS COME - BLESS HIS NAME!

Be ye at Peace - He is come -- Amen -- So be it and Selah --

I am He which is come - I am Sananda - Son of God -- Amen - So be it --

Sister Thedra of the Emerald Cross

They Plan A New Conquest

Sanat Kumara speaking:

Say unto them in the name of the Most High Living God that it is now come when the forces of darkness shall destroy themself ---

I say that when it is come that they have gone so far that they want the place wherein they have not set foot for their own - and wherein they shall be sent - they have gone too far!!

For they now plan a new conquest - they have been unto themself great torment - and they have labored long into the night that they might bring forth their "new plan"-- Yet 'my children' I say unto thee - great and wondrous is the way of the Lord ---

I bring unto thee a plan which is given unto US of the Hiarchi which <u>IS</u> and shall BE ---

I say that NONE shall set himself up as greater - I say he which tries is a fool indeed!

Blest is the meek and the lowly for he shall walk and talk with the emissaries of God -- They shall counsel with the ones which do sit in council for thy own welfare -- I say they shall have communication with God the Father -- Amen - so be it and Selah ---

I am revealed unto them which are prepared to receive me and of me - and I shall give unto them as they are prepared and they shall be glad -- So be it and Selah ---

I say they which do receive me shall be blest - they shall be as ones which have upon their head the Crown of the Sun and upon their forehead the Seal of Solomon -- So be it and Selah ---

I say they shall be brot out from the world of men and they shall be as ones prepared for the greater part -- So be it they shall sit upon the right hand of God the Father -- Amen and Selah ---

I say they shall not die -- Blest are they which do not die - for they shall be free forever and they shall go into darkness no more ---

I have said that they are being prepared as ye are - going about thy worldly affairs - and ye know it not - ye which are bound in darkness - Blest are they which are prepared for this day - for many shall ascend even as thy Lord - Sananda ---

Blest am I that I know Him - and I am glad - Amen -- So be it ye shall be blest as I am blest -- Amen and Amen ---

I am Sanat Kumara

Sister Thedra of the Emerald Cross

Bless them in Silence & Leave Them in Peace

Sanat Kumara speaking: -

Blest be this day - blest be they which call unto the Source of their being for knowledge - blest shall they be ---

Be ye as ones which has my hand upon thee and go into all the places wherein ye do go - as ones prepared to lift them up -

Give unto them nothing which shall stumble them - walk which way thy crown tilts not ---

Bless them in silence and leave them in peace and harmony -

Speak no word which is not prompted by Love - Peace and Harmony ---

Give unto them naught which they can use against thee - give unto them only that which shall bless them ---

Be ye as one which can comprehend that which I say unto thee ---

I say ye shall walk as the initiate upon the path - and ye shall NOT falter -- Woe unto him which faints and dies upon the path -- I say the path of initiation is strewn with the bones of the candidates for the greater part -- Blest are they which do receive the greater part - which ye do not find in thy libraries - in thy temples builded by man - nor within thy laboratories - for it is neither written nor spoken -- I say the greater part is neither written nor spoken ---

I say the Water of Life is of a truth the answer unto all thy woes - yet ye wait for this part ---

Too I say - it is a truth and it is recorded many times that all which do drink of the Water of Life which is liquid Light - shall receive the greater part for this is the plan of salvation - and it is my part at this time to reveal it unto them which are prepared to receive such revelation ---

Blest shall they be which are prepared -- I am with thee and I shall see thee thru thy trials and thy ordeals ---

Be ye blest of me and by me --

I am Sanat Kumara

Sister Thedra of the Emerald Cross

Transmutation of The Body

Sanat Kumara speaking: -

Sanat Kumara speaking unto thee on the subject of transmutation - ye have not as yet learned this law - yet ye shall ---

When one takes unto themself a body of earthly substance - for the purpose of bringing the octave of life down into the third dimension as flesh made manifest - they go thru a dimension of the etheric substance wherein matter exists as substance more dense than that of the fourth dimension - and then when they are finished with that substance of which is composed the third dimension vehicle - they are at once compelled by law to leave it behind or to transmute and take it with them -- When they transmute it it is placed upon them the responsibility of transmuting it - and when they accept the shield and the orb - they are as one which have gone the Royal Road ---

When they leave the vehicle of the third dimension behind - they are as ones which claim it in the years to come - which becomes their own responsibility - for it is the law that every atom which has been used by any personality within the Earth shall in time be transmuted and cleansed --

I say it shall be transmuted - for it is now come when ones which have misused the elements of the Earth shall be removed in their earthly vehicles - and others shall take upon themself the responsibility of transmuting their debris ---

So be it this shall be continued at a later time ---

I am Sanat Kumara

Sister Thedra of the Emerald Cross

Meet The Master
Add Not nor Take Away

Sanat Kumara speaking:-

Beloved of my being: Be ye blest of me and by me - and go ye into the place wherein ye shall go - as one prepared for that which shall be given unto thee to do ---

I say ye shall go into a place wherein ye have not been - and therein ye shall find one which has upon his head a crown - and upon his brow a countenance which is so bright ye cannot look upon it ---

Ye shall put thy hands over thy eyes and ye shall stand before him as one humble of heart -- Ye shall speak only that which is given unto thee to say - which is permitted by law - and ye shall not forget that which has been given unto thee to say - so long ago ---

I say ye shall have within thy own hand the key which shall be thy passport - and ye shall give it unto another which shall attend thee -- He shall call thy name and ye shall answer and ye shall be as one informed as to all the procedures---

Ye shall give this unto them and ye shall add naught - nor shall ye take away naught -- By the time they are prepared they shall have more and as they are prepared they shall be given that which is wise and prudent ---

Ye shall not add one word of thy own unto this document - for I say that which is wise and prudent - and I fear not - for I know whereof I speak - and I am not of a mind to betray myself --

There is a law which is given unto them at this point: "They which give of the word which is written unto the unlearned - the ones which have not prepared themself - shall be <u>by</u> <u>their</u> <u>own</u> <u>wonton</u> (willfulness) turned aside"- for they are not as yet responsible - nor are they worthy of the trust which is given unto the initiate - which is at all times trustworthy -- And ye shall know him by his acts - by his works - he goes not into the world - he does that which is given unto him to do with a glad heart - and a joyful heart beats within him - for the privilege of serving.

Blest are they which serve with a joyous heart - glad are they that they are here within this age ---

Be ye blest of me and of my presence --

I am Sanat Kumara

Sister Thedra of the Emerald Cross

Man's Potentials

Sarah speaking:

With my love do I enfold thee - with my hand shall I lead thee - and ye shall know me as I AM ---

Ye shall be as one brot out of bondage and ye shall be free forevermore - blest art thou for ye have asked that ye may have light -- Blest shall ye be ---

Art thou not given unto longing? and shall thy longing not be satisfied? I say all thy longing shall be satisfied -- So be it and Selah.

Great and mighty is the power which is within thy hand - yet ye have not known that which lies hidden therein -- I say ye shall come to know thyself as the one and only one -- Ye shall be as one come alive and ye shall be as one which has slept long - and which has been tormented by thy dreams ---

I say ye shall come alive - and ye shall wonder at thy slumbers - I say ye shall awaken - and glad ye shall be!

Blest are they which do awaken this day -- Amen and Selah -- Blessed are they for they shall see God face to face ---

Now ye shall know thy ONENESS with Him and ye shall separate thyself from Him no more ---

Great shall be thy power! for ye shall bring unto the altar that which has been willed unto thee of God the Father - and it shall be unto thee all things ---

Little have ye had for thine own - ye have rejected that which has been willed unto thee from the beginning -- Yet ye shall be glad for the little that ye have had - for it shall be increased - and ye shall stand as one unbound - as one prepared to receive thy inheritance in full -- So be it and Selah---

I am with thee unto the end -- Amen -- So be it and Selah

I am thy eternal Mother

Mother of Abraham

Sister Thedra of the Emerald Cross

...And All Things Shall Be Made New

Sanat Kumara speaking:-

Be ye blest of me and by me -- Give unto them this my word - even as it is given unto me of God our Father -- Bless them in His name - and go into the place wherein ye shall go as one prepared ---

Be ye as my hand made manifest this day - and for the first time I say unto them - they shall be given a part which is new unto them and they shall now prepare themself for this part - for it is now come when all the Earth shall go thru great change - and change shall be the key word in thy world - for not one shall stand still -- I say they either move forward or backward - and woe unto him which does not move with the stream of life - for they shall begin anew ---

Sad indeed is he which forfeits his inheritance ---

Be ye as my mouth made manifest and say unto them as I would say - that it is now come when they shall be uprooted - and they shall no longer sleep within their beds wherein they have slumbered as the weevil within the flour - he has been within the dark wherein he has spun his own web ---

Now it is come when thy nature shall be changed from the human to that of divine man - divinity man-ifested within the Earth -- And therein is the plan for all men within thy realm ---

Blest are they which do change their nature - I say none other changes it for thee ---

Be ye as one which has the will to prepare thyself - for not one can do it for thee - ye are thy own judge - thy own porter - thy own savior I have said many times: Ye shall receive as ye are prepared -- So be it and Selah ---

Now when ye have so prepared thyself - ye shall have a legion of light workers to aid thee in thy work - and ye shall be glad for their aid. Blest are they which do come unto thy aid - for it is for thy own good that they have left their places of light to come into thy world that ye may be aided at this time of great change -- I say ye shall no longer be within the places wherein ye have slept - ye shall be taken out - ye shall experience changes which are new unto thee - and for thy own sake shall ye be uprooted ---

Ye shall remember these my words and give thanks unto thy Source of being for all things - for it is now come when ye shall have one at thy side which is known as the Silent Watcher - and he shall not trespass upon thy free will - yet he shall direct thee and guide thee when ye do not know within thyself which way to go -- I say there shall be times when ye shall cry out: "My God - which way - which way" ---

Blest are they which turn unto the Source -- Be ye as one which has heard me - and blest shall ye be -- I come that ye may be blest ---

I am Sanat Kumara

Sister Thedra of the Emerald Cross

The Great White Altar … The Sponsor

Sananda speaking: -

Beloved of my being: Be ye blest of me and by me -- Yes shall now place thy hand on mine and I shall lead thee into the place wherein I shall take thee - and I shall give unto thee as ye are prepared to receive And I say ye have prepared thyself for this day - and ye shall be glad for thy preparation -- So be it and Selah ---

Blest are they which are prepared - blest shall they be -- Be ye as one which has been true unto thy own self and unto thy trust - for it is now come when one shall come unto thee and he "shall bring thee into the place wherein I am - and therein ye shall find that which ye have written with thy own hand - and ye shall find it upon the Altar of White Alabaster - whereupon ye shall find written the symbol which has been given unto thee - and therein many things shall be revealed unto thee.

Too I say - great shall be thy revelation and great shall be thy strength - and blest shall ye be- for I say unto thee ye shall be as one made new and ye shall be as one come alive - for it is now come when ye shall stand before the Great White Altar - and one shall declare for thee thy freedom - forever free from all bounds - and therein is wisdom therein is thy freedom - for within that which is given unto the Father - is ours to have and to hold -- Forever are we free within Him - which is our heritage - therein is our "Sonship" our Godhood -- Amen - so be is and be it so ----

For the first time I say unto thee - ye shall be called at the hour of midnite and ye shall answer -- And one shall take thee out - and ye shall have no fear - nor shall ye faint - for ye shall have my hand upon thee and I shall bear thee up - and ye shall have that which I have promised thee - and I say thy reward shall be great indeed -- So be it and Selah.

I am thy Sibor and thy Brother - Sananda

Sister Thedra of the Emerald Cross

Patience & Dignity – Obedience

Sananda speaking: -

Beloved of my being: Be ye blest of my presence - for I come unto thee that ye may be blest -- Have I not given unto thee this part that they may receive of me - thru thee? Blest are they which shall receive of me thru thee - and blest shall ye be -- For this do I give unto thee a new part - that they may be blest of me thru thee ---

While it is come that they are in the place wherein they shall prepare themself - they shall be as ones which shall count the days while they serve within that place with patience and with dignity -- Yet I say they shall count the days - for they are but few indeed - for they shall be brot out from their places wherein they are and shall be for a time - a very short while ---

And while they do remain within their places wherein they now are they shall cultivate patience and dignity - they shall be glad for that which they are given to do -- They shall find them which are fortuned to be prepared to receive as they have received - and they shall walk as <u>becoming</u> - before them which shall be brot in - and they shall not put before them a stumbling block ---

I say ye shall give unto them which have asked for this part - these my words which I have given unto thee for them ---

Now I say - one among them shall be brot out and she shall come into the place wherein ye are for a time - and she too shall go into the Great White Mountain wherein stands the Great White Altar of Alabaster ---

I say not one - but two shall go into the mountain wherein they shall find one which is known as Sananda - which shall speak the word which shall free them from all bondage forever ---

I say that they know not which is fortuned them - blest shall they be -- I know that which they shall do and that which shall be given unto them ---

Now ye shall say unto them in my name that they have done exceedingly well - yet they have not gone into t of the Most High -- I say they have not as yet received the greater part - for this have they waited -- Blest shall they be - for they shall see me face to face ---

I am Sananda

Sister Thedra of the Emerald Cross

Ye Are Not of the Old Order

Sarah Speaking : -

Beloved of my being: Be ye as one blest - for I reveal myself unto thee for that purpose - that ye may go into the place of the Most High Living God as one prepared - that ye may know me as I know thee - that ye may receive thy inheritance in full - that ye may be brot in - into the place from which ye went out - within this day -- For this have I revealed myself unto thee ---

Now it is come when they which are of a mind shall receive me unto themself - and they shall be as ones blest - for <u>they</u> shall be brot home and they shall go into darkness no more - for this is the New Day the new dispensation - and for this has the new dispensation been given thee ---

Now again it shall be recorded: "Ye are no longer under the old law nor are ye of the old order - ye ha a new dispensation and a new law" and the fullness of these things shall be revealed unto them which are of a mind to receive me and of me -- Blest are they for I shall speak with them and I shall give unto them as they are prepared to receive.

Before ye were - there was a place wherein ye began – wherein ye had thy beginning upon the Earth - and I say ye were within another place before the world was -- Before the Earth was prepared - ye had yet another place - then ye chose to come into the Earth - that it might become as a place for the Sons of God - and ye have come as martyr - as saint - as sinner - as harlot - as master -- Ye have taken upon thyself all the colors of man - Faye have taken many paths - ye have spoken all languages - ye have been thru the greatest of temples -- Ye have led them which came ye have been led by the great and the near great - and ye have grown old -- Ye have been given the key - ye have lost it -- Ye now shall re-discover it and ye shall find it within thyself - blest is he which does find it for it lies buried deep within him

While it is yet time - I shall say unto thee - ye shall have all the assistance, necessary - that ye might discover the secret place wherein ye may have thy head unbound and thy hands untied - for many have come into thy Earth to assist thee at this time - and they tire not - nor do they FORCH (force) upon thee that which ye are not prepared to receive - they are discreet - prudent and just in all their ways they are in all ways just and prudent -- They give not their pearls of price unto babes which know not their worth ---

Be ye at peace this day - and give unto me credit for that which I AM - and I shall speak with thee in the hours of thy sleep -- Be ye blest of my presence for I AM - thy Mother Eternal

Sister Thedra of the Emerald Cross

Personality & Free Will

Sarah speaking - Beloved children: -

O my children: Call upon me thy Mother - that ye may fix thy mind thy thots upon me - that I might touch thee - that I might speak to thee that ye may take time to listen for my words -- Say unto thyself: I AM I KNOW I AM - and for this I have a Source and I shall give thot unto it - the Cause of my being ---

O my children - I speak unto thee - ye turn thy face from me and remember me not -- Be ye mindful of me and I shall give unto thee a part which I have kept for thee - and ye shall have cause for rejoicing.

Blest are they which see me - and which remember their being with me -- I say - great shall be the joy of them which return unto me - for they shall be made new - and they shall be reborn -- Born of God the Father shall they be and they shall receive their Godhood - their orb and their scepter - and they shall be Gods within their own right - for He thy Father has willed it so -- So be it and Selah ---

Praise ye the name of Solen - from which ye have gone out - for none other is above Him - none other has given unto thee being - and ye have turned thy face from Him - ye have remembered Him not -- Ye have been asleep - lo the times and half times - ye have gone into the realms of darkness in thy slumbers ---

Ye have gone into embodiment many times and ye have not as yet awakened unto thy own inheritance - for it is a glorious inheritance which ye have forfeited while ye have slept -- I have waited thy return and I am now prepared to receive thee unto myself - and I say - be ye of a mind to return unto me - and I shall send one unto thee which shall give unto thee a portion which shall be unto thee all things - which shall be unto thee the Water of Life -- I say ye shall now decide for thyself which way ye go - and blest are they which return this day unto me ---

I am thy Mother Eternal - I am the fortune of thy Father God - which has given unto thee being - and ye know me not - yet for that which I am ye have been given being - ye have been given expression and ye have been given personality -- Ye have gone out from me as a personality unlike another and ye have been given free will - and I say unto thee - ye have misused it for thy own sake - for thy own end -- Now it is time that ye use it for thy own salvation ---

I say unto thee my children: Arise - come unto me and I shall give unto thee rest from all thy woes - all thy cares -- I shall give unto thee peace as ye have not known -- Blest are they which know such peace - for they shall know God the Father -- At no time shall ye be turned away -- Be ye aware of me - of my presence - and I shall lead thee into the place wherein ye shall abide with me -- I am thy Mother

Sister Thedra of the Emerald Cross

The Unknown Helpers

Sanat Kumara speaking: -

Sarah - our Mother - has spoken unto thee -- From out the depth of her heart has she called unto thee and her - yet ye have not comprehended the depth of her love - nor have ye been in the place wherein she abides - since thy going out from her ---

She has now spoken unto thee that ye might return unto her this day I say she shall speak unto thee again this day - and she shall give unto thee that which shall profit thee - and ye shall be blest by her and of her.

I am now with thee that ye may be prepared to receive her -- And too - I am come that ye may be prepared to receive one which shall come as a Brother -- And he has as yet not spoken unto thee - for he has as yet not been within thy own realm - he has been in the secret place of the Most High Living God ---

I say unto thee - he has not been in the Earth - he is not of Earth nor has he taken embodiment in any other worlds - he is now entering into the world of flesh made manifest for the first time ---

I say ye know little of that which goes on round and about thee - for they do work among thee unknown unto thee ---

Ye shall now walk with them and talk with them - and ye shall be glad for thy knowing - such is wisdom ---

Be ye prepared - for this one shall come unto thee and he shall counsel thee and he shall be unto thee much light - and blest shall ye be ---

I am with thee and I shall not forsake thee - such is my mission ---

I am thy Brother and thy Sibor - Sanat Kumara

Sister Thedra of the Emerald Cross

Diligence & Obedience

Sananda speaking:-

Beloved of my being: Ye have now come unto this altar for the purpose of asking for light and ye shall be as one which has been heard and answered - for I say a host shall reveal unto thee many things - and ye shall go out as one prepared that ye may give unto them as ye have received ---

Blest are they which prepare themself for the greater part

Now when ye have gone out from the place wherein ye are ye shall be as one prepared for the greater part ---

Now ye have been within the place wherein ye are as one which has the first part - and ye have been diligent and obedient in all thy ways - yet ye have not received the greater part - ye comprehend not the fullness of thy inheritance - for ye have as yet not been glorified as He would have thee ---

I say ye as yet have not been glorified -- Blest are they which are glorified in the Father for ye shall be as one reborn of God the Father - and ye shall stand face to face with Him -- So be it and Selah ---

Wherein is it written that there are none so foolish as he which thinks himself wise? Wherein is it written that when ye are wise ye shall know the law governing thy being?

Be ye as one true unto thy own self and ask of the Father that ye may have such knowledge -- Blest are they which ask for they shall be heard -- Will ye not ask for thy inheritance? Will ye not receive even as I have received? I have spoken and ye have heard me --So be it and Selah --

Was it not said that one should speak unto thee? And it is now come when ye shall receive of this one which has waited f this day when he may speak unto one which is prepared to receive him and of him - and he shall be unto thee great light ---

For the first time he speaks unto one from out the realms of light - he comes for the first time since the door has been opened tween thy world and his - for this has he waited ---

Belearian is now with thee and he shall speak as I speak and ye shall receive him in the name of the Father - Son and Holy Ghost -- Amen and Selah ---

Belearian

Belearian speaking: Was it not given unto thee to be prepared for this part even before ye took embodiment thru woman - and have ye not been with me even before ye were born of woman? I say unto thee - ye have had thy beginning in the realm of Light - therein is thy salvation.

I say ye are - and ye are one with me - for I am not of the nether world - nor are ye of the nether world - ye are of God the Father - even as I -- Ye have come into the Earth many times that ye might add thy light unto that of the others - sent even as I am sent -- I am sent of God the Father that there might be a gathering in - "A gathering In"---

And I say the harvest shall be great - for it is the day of awakening when many shall awake and they shall wonder why they have slept so long -- Be blest to be part of this age - of this new dispensation ---

I say unto thee my hand made manifest: - that within the mountain which towers over thee that they are prepared within it -- They which are of the Council shall bring thee in as ones which are prepared - to sibor and to prepare thee for the Day of Judgement ---

Now remember ye this - "There are none so foolish as the one which thinks himself wise!"---

For within the Great White Mountain sits a Council which is prepared for this day - and not far off is the day when the door unto the temple therein shall swing wide unto the ones which are prepared to enter therein - I say blest is he which so prepares himself ---

Now let it be said and recorded that there are none so foolish as he which betrays himself or his trust - and he which does is the greatest of fools ---

Now be ye prepared to receive me and of me - and I shall come unto thee again and give unto thee a part which shall be new unto thee ---

I am thy Sibor and thy older Brother – Belearian

Sister Thedra of the Emerald Cross

The <u>Silent</u> Watchers

Sanat Kumara speaking: -

Blest are they which serve as the silent watchers - blest are they which receive the silent watchers - and ye are part of such an one ---

I say they which have such responsibility are not without reward - for they shall be blest indeed ---

Be ye at the altar at an hour when they may come together for the part which shall be given unto them --- (WAIT)

Sanat Kumara returning that ye may again be blest - that ye may come unto this altar for the purpose of such communication - blest are they which do ask for such communication ---

Now ye shall be reminded of thy blessings - and from whence they cometh ---

I am he which is responsible for thy welfare at this time - for it is my responsibility to bring into manifestation this temple - and to provide for it - yet I say ye shall be my servants - ye shall be my hands made manifest - my feet made manifest ---

Ye shall be blest accordingly - ye shall be filled unto thy capacity - and ye shall be blest by the ones which ye have looked unto for thy strength -- "Thy Benefactors which are thy older Brothers - which have gone before ye that ye might not trip over the pitfalls - such is their love their life - that they turn to give unto thee a hand"-- I say ye shall turn when ye have reached the summit and give unto thy brother a hand which comes after thee -- For this do I now reach out my hand unto thee that ye too may enter into the Holy of Holies ---

Blest are they which do reach the summit - glad shall they be -- Ye have as yet not reached it within this realm - ye have as yet not gained thy freedom -- For this do I reach out my hand that ye may reach thy appointed goal -- For this have ye come into this realm of man at this time ---

Praise God the Father Eternal for His Love - Mercy and Wisdom - that He has given unto thee a new dispensation this day ---

I say ye shall will it so that it be finished - that ye may find thy way into the place from whence ye went out - and that ye be eternally free from all bondage forever - and that ye may go into darkness no more - I am glad for this day - for I have waited long that I might come unto thee thusly --

I am thy Sibor and thy older Brother - Sanat Kumara

Sister Thedra of the Emerald Cross

There are "Watchers" and "Silent Watchers"

The Power of Speech

Sanat Kumara speaking:

Might are the WORDS of God the Father - Might are His WORKS! Blest are they which speak the words which are of Him - The Father -- Blest are they which do the work of the Father -- Blest are they which know the law governing speech ---

Blest shall they be which use the gift of speech for that which shall bless all mankind - for as the fowls of the air return unto their roosting places - So shall thy words return unto thee - either to bless or to torment thee ---

Be ye aware of thy tongue - it can be a dangerous thing indeed -- Be ye as wise as the serpent and silent as the Sphinx

Blest are they which do know when speech is necessary - for it is the breath of God which is used -- Be ye mindful of thy mis-use of the power of speech - for it is in no wise necessary to answer the foolish - be ye no part of an argument which is given unto the foolish ---

Bless them which mis-use thee and give unto them nothing which they can use against thee - I say give them nothing which they can mis-use -- Bless them for that which they are - and not for that which they appear to be ---

Be ye as ones which know the law - and abide by it - I say - be no part of their smallness - their pettiness - and go in and out among them with love in thy heart and joy within thee -- And go into the places wherein ye shall go - as ones alert and mindful of thy own affairs - and question not them of theirs ---

Be ye as one which is filled with love - and give unto them of thy love - and give not of thy energy unto frivolity - for it is not necessary to be unbecoming unto them ---

I say ye shall walk as one which has a crown upon thy head - and walk which way it tilts not - and blest shall ye be---

I am thy Brother and thy Sibor - Sanat Kumara

Sister Thedra of the Emerald Cross

The Prodigal (Memory) <u>Son</u>

Sarah speaking -

Beloved children which has gone out from me - I am as thou art - I am with thee - I am thee -

I am not separated from thee - Ye are separated from me - Because ye have had thy memory blanked from thee –

Ye have not remembered me - Ye have not given unto thyself credit for being my son - daughter - Ye have given unto the Source of thy being little thought -

Ye have wandered in darkness to the eons of time - Now ye shall arise and come home -

I say - I have called thee home - For the first time in thy history have I ordered thee home - Ye have been given a new dispensation - a new law - and ye are no longer under the old law -

Ye are under the new dispensation which is fashioned within the inner temple for thy own sake -

I command thee my children - Arise - Alert thyself and return unto me this day - Bless them which do return this day - for they shall be as ones returned unto their abiding place -

Be ye as ones which hear me and give heed unto that which I say unto thee and ye shall go into darkness no more -

Blest are they which do receive me - For ye shall be free forevermore -

Be ye as one which has gone out from me and which has returned unto me – And great shall be thy joy - Amen and Selah -

I am thy SOUL - thy BREATH - I AM THYSELF MADE MANIFEST - So be it and Selah -

I am Sarah - Mother of Abraham -

Sister Thedra of the Emerald Cross

Sanat Kumara speaking -

Beloved of my being - Ye shall say unto them as I would say that within the time which is near they shall be given a part which is new unto them and they shall be as ones called out of their beds at the midnight hour - when they shall be unprepared -

Too I say, this is the day of preparation - when they shall prepare themself for their new part - And within the time which is near they shall be brought into the place wherein I am and prepared for the greater part - They which have prepared themself for this part -

They which are not prepared shall be caught up short of their course.

Be ye as ones alert - And do not overlook the keys - For I say unto thee I am mindful of thy plight - And of thy weakness - And I am not so foolish as to betray my trust -

I have been sent that ye might be brought out - And for this does this Council labor day and night - For thy own sake - Ye know <u>not</u> that ye are standing on the threshold of thy new place of abode -

Ye shall NOT stand still! I say ye either move forward or ye go backward - There is no stopping place - There is no pause - There is only progression -

Yet the one which does not have the mind to learn shall be put into his own environment - wherein there shall be a sifting - And from that place there shall again be ones lifted up - ones taken out - and prepared again - They shell be given as they are prepared to receive -

None go unrewarded - They receive according to their preparation.

Now - Wherein is it written that "There are none so foolish as the one which betrays himself" - And it is indeed a truth -

This is the Day of Salvation -- And when ye have been given the keys - in little while and with few words - Ye shall be wise to use them for we of the eternal realms are not given unto preachments - We are NOT given to many words - For we are of the mind to enlighten thee in little time and with great love - and in wisdom - We are efficient in all things -

Be ye blest to receive us and of us - For I say the Mighty Council of the Seven Lights now is in session for thy own well-being. Each day ones come and goes which are of other realms - realms of Light - wherein they are free - Yet others stay within the council chambers for long periods of time where in others join them for such as is to be done -

Some from among thee are brought in for counselling and are then returned unto their own environment - While this is being accomplished they which walk in darkness are in darkness still - Bless them for that which they are and give un to them no condemnation - Be ye a living example of the initiate and walk among them as such - I am thy Sibor and thy older brother - Sanat Kumara

Sister Thedra of the Emerald Cross

Sanat Kumara speaking:

Was it not said in the beginning that the word was God - And the word was with God - And from the beginning was it so - So be it and Selah -

For the first time it is given unto the child of earth the power which has been held in trust for this day - Now ye have thought thyself wise indeed and ye have given unto thyself credit for being wise -

Yet ye have no idea of that which is in store for thee - Nor do ye ask of God the Father - Ye are not of a mind to learn of Him - Ye learn from trial and error and ye are as ones which have upon thy own shoulders great responsibility - for it is now come when ye have set into motion great forces which shall devour thee -

Ye shall be consumed by thy own ambition for power and for thy own greatness shall ye perish -

None escapes the law - And wherein is it written that ye shall receive as ye are prepared -

Now it is written that when one goes into the dragon's den he shall be as one which goes into the place where angels fear to tread - He shall find therein many pitfalls which have been carefully lain to beguile him. He shall find therein many which shall call him just and wise - He shall be as one puffed up of his <u>own</u> greatness and he shall call himself great and just for his own gratification - And I say unto him - Oh thou fool! For pity is he!

Now I say unto them which do sit in high places - Be ye as the fools which have thy fingers within thy ears and thy head bound - Ye see not, neither do ye hear that which is said unto thee - I say Oh ye braggards, ye hypocrites - Ye which do speak with tongues of angels and belie thy words - Ye hypocrites - ye fools! Hear me - hear me - for I am now come that ye may hear me - I say it shall end - this thy idolatory, thy hypocrisy which is an abomination in the sight of God the Father - I say ye shall depart from out the offices of the people - Ye shall unbind them - Ye shall be unto them their oppressor no longer! Ye shall be as ones bound by that which ye have bound - I say ye shall unbind the people which ye have bound - Be ye alert and give unto them their liberty and pray that thy freedom be given unto thee -

I say ye have held forth for the last time - I say thy day is come and thy reign is ended - Yet it shall be as one has said before me - that the day of judgement is now come -

I say ye are now this day writing thy own passport into thy next place of abode - Ye choose this day that which ye shall do - for I say ye have the free will endowed unto thee of God the Father - and not even He shall trespass upon it - Ye possess naught else for not even the air ye breathe is thine - Not even the chemical components of thy body is thine - Ye have nothing! Nothing!

And yet ye lay claim unto the land - the seas - Ye conquest thy way into the ether - Ye conquest thy way into all the lands of earth and ye set up boundaries and mark them well - And inter state lines and outer state lines - Ye place great and impressive monuments at thy lines and place guards therein and ye are inclined to hatred and ye preach from thy altars which ye have set up patriotic sermons which are designed to send thy sons into battle. Ye prepare them for battle. Ye give unto them medals for taking from their brothers their vehicles - Ye give unto them the weapons of war and give unto them medals for expertness in their use - I say ye violators - ye fools - Thy day is ended - Ye shall find thyself tormented by many plagues - many pestilences - Many storms shall beset thy shores -

Many of thy war ships shall find their way unto the depth of both seas - Many of the airlines shall close their doors - Many of thy air ships shall take with them the lives of thousands of people - I say recon with the host -

Consider well the law, for it is neigh time when ye shall be brought face to face with thy foolishness - Consider well thy own responsibility for ye have forgotten from whence ye came and ye know not whither thou goest -

Be ye wise and hear that which I say unto thee and ye shall be as one which has upon thy shoulders the responsibility of thy own life - for thy own deeds - I say none escape the law -

I have spoken and ye shall -- hear me --

Amen - So be it - I am Sanat Kumara - Son of God the Father

Sister Thedra of the Emerald Cross

Wherein?

Sarah speaking -

Beloved children of earth - Wherein have I turned thee away - ?

Wherein have I denied thee - ?

Wherein have I cut thee off from me - ?

Wherein have ye given unto me credit for being thy Mother eternal, Wherein have ye ask that ye return unto me?

Now ye shall bring thyself unto this altar as ones prepared to receive me - And of me - For I shall open wide the door which shall make it possible to return unto me -

I shall call forth the living flame which shall burn upon thy own altar -wherein ye shall dwell with me forever - I shall call forth from myself that which has animated thy soul. And I shall give unto thee that which has been willed unto thee of God the Father and ye shall dwell in the House of the Living God forever more -

Because I AM thou art - And ye have been given thy being thru me and of me and ye have as yet not remembered me - For this do I come that ye may -

Blest are they which do remember me and their being which they have had with me -

Forgive thyself thy unknowing and be ye as one which can turn from thy old way and turn thy face homeward - And ye shall be forgiven of all thy old ways - All thy unknowing - All thy wonton and ye shall be healed of thy blindness and of thy deafness -

Ye shall be healed of all thy infirmities and ye shall return unto me Perfect even as ye went out from me - So be it the Fathers will -

I am now prepared to bring thee home and there shall be great joy wherein the ones await to receive thee - Blest are they which return this day. I have spoken - Ye have heard - Ye have born witness of me this day.

Praise the Source of thy being - In all things give thanks - Give unto God the Father Praise for all that He has <u>caused</u> to be accomplished within this temple and ye shall be blest according unto thy capacity to receive -

I am thy Mother eternal

Praise Praise - Sing unto Him a joyful song -

Santos Archi Modra Padre-Beautiful - Salicea -

Sister Thedra of the Emerald Cross

Sananda speaking -

Beloved of my being - Blest art thou and blest shall ye be - I come unto thee that ye may be blest - and that ye may be brot out of bondage.

Ye shall now give unto me credit for knowing that which I say unto thee - And ye shall remember that which I say - And ye shall be wise to heed that which I say - For it is for thy own welfare and I say ye shall do well to alert thyself and be up and about thy preparation - Have ye not slept on thy feet - And have ye not gone into lethargy - I say ye are not yet strong enough to stand on thy own two feet - Ye are as ones bound and ye have not yet the strength to stand alone -

And for that do I stand ready to unbind thee - To give unto thee as ye are prepared to receive - I say as ye prepare thyself so shall ye receive - Ye are as ones which have gone unto the fountain with a small container - Yes perish for foresight - Ye ask not that ye be directed in all thy ways - Ye go into the hi-ways and by-ways as one on whose shoulders rest great responsibility -

Ye are not prone to knowledge - Ye are asleep and know it not -

Ye are as yet bound by flesh - Ye are NOT free -

I am within the world of men - Yet I am not of the world - I am not bound by my body - I am free from all bounds -

I can use the elements for that which I will for I know the law - And I abide by it - Such is wisdom - So be it ye shall come to know the law governing the elements and ye shall be true unto thy trust and ye shall be glad - So be it and Selah -

I am the Brother and thy servant -

Sananda - Son of God the Father - Amen - So be it and be it so -

Solen Solen Aum Solen -

Praise be unto thee

Sori Sori -

Sister Thedra of the Emerald Cross

Bor speaking -

Sori Sori Sori -

Praise unto the Father God -

Praise the name of Solen forever and forever - Praise the Father-Mother God forever more -

By their GRACE and their mercy shall ye be brought out of bondage - And for this have ye waited - By thy own effort shall ye prepare thyself that ye may be delivered out -

Wherein is it written "None takes thee out - Against thy will"

Be ye of a mind to return unto thy abiding place and ye shall be delivered out forever and forever. So be it and be it so - Amen and Selah.

By thy own efforts shall ye be delivered - I say ye and ye alone are thy ones which hold thyself bound - For nothing can hold thee against thy will -

Because ye have followed the dragon - And because ye are of a mind to serve him are ye held in bondage - Ye have served him with all thy might - All thy time - All thy strength have ye devoted unto him -

Little time have ye give unto thy own deliverance - for ye separate thyself from the Source of thy being - Ye go in and out the dragons den with little thought of thy God - thy divinity - Ye forget that ye have been offered thy freedom - Ye forget what has been said unto thee from the realms of light -

Ye forget not that which <u>they</u> say unto thee - Ye fret and cry over that which <u>they</u> say - And ye turn thy face from the Source -

Ye call out for help from them and they hear thee - yet they do not deliver thee out - For they are yet in darkness - They are as thou art - Bound within the dragons den - They serve him and know it not -

Now will ye not seek thy Source of Being and return unto it -

Be not bound by opinions and the puny will of man - for it is as a millstone upon thy back -

Ye shall free thyself of all thy opinions and of thy own leg-irons -

Be ye of a <u>mind</u> to learn - Lay aside thy old pre-conceived ideas - Use thy own free will that ye may be unbound - And let no man say which way ye shall go -

Forgive them which would bind thee and give unto them NO power to hold thee -

I say ye battle against them - Yet ye need NOT -

For thy own will to be unbound shall be thy shield and thy buckler.

Be ye as one which has the mind to comprehend that which I say unto thee -

Go thy way in Peace and thanksgiving and bless this day - For it is now come when ye shall come to know many things which ye have not known since ye went into darkness -

Ye are fortuned to be within the earth at this time for a great and divine plan -

I am with thee unto the end -

I am thy older brother and thy Sibor -

Bor -

Sister Thedra of the Emerald Cross

Sarah speaking -

While ye are yet bund within the earthly vehicle ye shall be as one which has thy hand in mine and I shall lead thee from out thy bondage.

I shall give unto thee as ye are prepared to receive -

I shall give unto thee as a Mother gives unto the child - And I shall be as thy Mother eternal - I shall not deceive thee - nor shall I deny thee.

I shall bestow upon my love and all that I have - I shall bless thee with my being - I shall hold thee fast in the hours of thy trial - I shall bless thee with my very being -

I shall speak unto thee in the hours of thy sleep - I shall cause thee to remember that which I have said - I shall await thy return unto me and I shall be glad for thy return -

Bring unto the altar thy heart - thy hands as a living sacrifice - that ye may purchase thy own passport into the place wherein I am - For naught else shall redeem thyself - When it is come that ye surrender up thyself - A host of light workers shall come unto thee for the purpose of assisting thee in thy flight - Such is their part -

Yet ye shall do thy part - that is of preparing thyself for to receive them - So be it thy part -

I say unto thee - Be ye true unto thyself and turn thy face homeward. For it is now come when great shall be thy work which shall be given unto thee to do - And great shall be thy responsibility -

For many shall turn unto thee and ask of thee the way - I say many come unto thee to ask of thee the way -

And they shall be heard and answered - So be it and Selah -

I am come that they may be answered - So be it and Selah -

I am thy Mother Sarah - Mother of Abraham -

Sister Thedra of the Emerald Cross

Sananda speaking -

Blest art thou o my children - I come unto thee as thou hast come that there might be light within the world of man - I say that there might be light in the world of man -

For it is now come when they have forgotten their Source of being. And they are not of a mind to see the light within the Father's realm -

They run to and fro and seek within dark places for wisdom - wherein is no wisdom - and the law prevents them from that which they strive to attain -

I say they shall find no wisdom - No Peace - Until they turn unto the Source of their being - Blest are they which do turn unto Him - God the Father -

That which was given unto them in ages past that they may comprehend such laws as govern the earth and the elements have been misused --<u>Mis</u>-interpreted - And they have been adulterated - And they have been given unto the unjust and imprudent - They have added to and taken from them - Until now - there is little left which would be unto thee of any value -

I say ye have not had the records revealed unto thee - Ye have been as ones running hither and yon - Seeking wisdom - Ye have not sought thy freedom in the realms of light -

Ye are blinded by thy own simple foolishness - Ye are in the thinkers realm - Ye are as ones u<u>n</u>-enlightened - Ye <u>know</u> not -

For the law governing the elements shall be held in trust for the day when they are prepared to use it for the good of all mankind -

I say ye shall not conquest the planets of thy solar system -

Ye shall not pilfer the plans which has been held for the initiate -

Ye shall not betray the Hiarchi - Ye may betray thyself - NOT the Hiarchi -

The Father has given unto the children of earth the new dispensation which is designed to free thee - Yet ye make laws to bind them - Ye make weapons which are designed to destroy them - Ye are as judge which sit in high places - Ye are as the parrots - Ye parrot thy sayings - thy opinions - Ye are as bigots - Ye are hypocrits - Ye sell and barter the tools of Satan - Ye are of the mind to serve him -

Ye are not of a mind to turn from him - Ye go into the dragons den with thy hand out - Ye go into the places set aside as the temple of the Living God - Ye wear thy mask - Ye wear thy gaudy clothing - Ye care not for thy poor - Ye care not for the suffering -

I say thy penny is of no value - Ye cannot buy thy way into the Kingdom of God -

Ye give thy penny of no value - While ye withhold thy love and thyself - I say again give unto God the Father - Thy Heart - thy hand - thy will -

Many go into the places wherein they lie dying - They fear to touch them - They shudder at the stench -

They refrain from going because they cannot bear the sight of them which are sick - blind - lame and deaf - Them which are their brothers They fear for themself -

Why Oh why are ye so blind - Why are ye so doleful

Ye indulge thyself - Ye give not of thyself -

When - Oh children will ye awaken - I stand with hands tied - I cry unto thee in the name of our Father which has sent me unto thee - AWAKEN AWAKEN - I am come that ye might awaken - I say unto ye sleeper - Many are ascending unto the Father this day as ones freed from all bondage forever - free forever free and ye know it not -

Ye sleep on - On Father I have come into the earth at thy will - Why do they not know me - Oh Father cause them to awaken! Thy will be done for them thru me, thy Son - Amen - So be it and be it so -

I am Sananda -

Hallajula - Amen

Praise His Holy Name -

Sister Thedra of the Emerald Cross

Sori Sori - Bor speaking -

Blest be ye this day - Blest am I that I am prepared to come unto thee thusly - for I am of the Father sent that ye may have light -

Poor in spirit are they which do not receive of the light - for they cut themself off without the substance of life -

Poor in spirit are they which turn from their Source - Poor in spirit are they which think themself wise - They shall be found without substance -

I am sent of God the Father that ye may have light - I come unto thee as one qualified of Him-the Father that I might give unto thee a guiding hand - I have worked in silence lo the many centuries - from the time of my initiation within the land of the Andes wherein I was prepared for my ascension by many of the great initiates - Our beloved brother Maher being the Grand Master within the temple of Panamanche - Wherein many ascended even as I -

Now I shall relate for them which are fortuned to read these words my own ascension - which was from the beginning part of this plan -

When I was a young man of mature age I lived on the west side or shore of Africa wherein flourished a great and grand civilization which has been lost in antiquity - Ye have no knowledge of its beauty and science - for from it grew many branches which are likewise lost to mankind -

When it came that I was prepared for this part of my preparation for the "Greater Part" I was brought thru the interior of the earth - called the "Inner Way" - And we entered that great and glorious temple of Panamanche on the island of Terrawatta of the Andes Mountains - Now ye - My sister Thedra - shall remember my account given on that place wherein ye recorded the first account which was given unto thee -

Ye were within that place called Terrawatta with me at the time of my ascension - Ye saw that part of my preparation - this account is part of that which was given unto thee to be done at this time - Ye accepted this part - And it is as yet not finished - For it is near time when again we shall come together face to face and ye shall remember me and it shall seem as a day since that great day when we stood upon the great golden altar and received the blessings of our beloved and blessed brother Sanat Kumara - which was even then the Comanche - Be ye blest of him as I have been blest -

I shall bring unto thee one which shall speak with thee at a later hour - I am prepared to speak at that time -

I am Bor -

Sister Thedra of the Emerald Cross

Bor speaking -

Blessings from the throne of the Most High Living God - Be ye blest of me and of my presence -

I come unto thee as one prepared for to give thee as I have received of the Father-Mother God -

I declare for thee that which the Father has willed unto thee - I declare for thee that which is thy rightful inheritance -

I declare for thee that which is thine by direct inheritance - I say ye are the children of God the Father - and none shall deny thee thy inheritance - which is willed unto thee -

Ye shall now declare for thyself that which is thy own by divine right and direct inheritance - Ye shall be as ones prepared to receive that which has been kept for thee for this day -

Ye have forfeited thy inheritance - Yet ye shall now claim it and ye shall be as ones prepared to receive it and ye shall be glad -

For it is now come when ye shall come to know thy own power and thy own power which has been held concealed within thy own flame shall be revealed unto thee -

Ye shall have the power revealed unto thee when ye have proven thyself worthy of such power - And none shall put within thy hand the rod and the staff before ye are prepared to use it with love, wisdom and justice - I say as ye are prepared - So shall ye receive - Be ye as ones prepared for the Greater Part -

Now ye shall come to know that which is meant by the Greater Part For ye which are prepared shall be participants in the great and grand plan - which is brought forth thru the Hiarchi and when ye have prepared thyself to receive such revelations ye shall be brought into the secret place - wherein we which sit in council for thy benefit do dwell and wherein we do keep vigil for thy safety - and I wherein ye shall sit in council for the benefit of all mankind - and wherein ye shall have the laws expounded and revealed - and ye shall see the wisdom of thy preparation - and ye shall rejoice that this day is come -

Praise His Holy Name - Solen Solen - Aum Solen -

Be ye as one which has my hand upon thee and I shall bless thee - and I shall stand ready to assist thee - Call and I shall answer thee for I do hear thee and I come at thy call -

I say forget not the cause of thy being and forget not thy benefactors which are sent to assist thee - I am thy servant in the name of the Most High Living God -

Amen and Selah - I am Bor -

Sister Thedra of the Emerald Cross

Blest are they which come unto this altar in the name of the Father Son and Holy Ghost - Amen - So be it -

I come that ye may have light - I come that ye may be brout out of bondage - I come that ye may return unto thy abiding place - I am come that ye may know as I know - I am come that ye may be even as I AM.

And I am One with the Father-Mother God - I AM - And I know myself to be -

I have not separated myself from them - I am one with them and I AM - for that part not of a mind to separate myself from them - I go not out from them - Neither do I take upon myself a body of flesh substance. I am eternally a virgin - I create not - Neither am I created - I AM - have been and always shall be -

I was before Abraham was and I shall be when all the galaxies shall pass from their spheres - I AM - And I am nameless - I AM formless - I AM soundless - Yet I AM all these things without me there would be No-thing - I AM that I AM - Ye name it and that I AM -

I come not - Neither do I go - I AM ever present - I AM the beginning and the end - Yet I have no beginning and I have no end - I am neither male or female - I am neither black or white -

I am not confined to any sphere - Neither am I confined unto any octave - Any part of any system - no galaxy - No place contains me - No part binds me - I AM freedom - I AM boundless -

I AM neither great - nor small - I AM all that which is REAL - I AM - I AM - And ever shall be -

I AM because I AM and none shall limit me by naming me - Yet I am called by many names - NO man knows me - for I AM the unknown. The unknown which is UN-knowable - I AM the Alpha and Omega - I go within - I go without - I am within - I AM without - Yet I go not - Neither do I come - I AM -

I give not - Neither do I take - I need not for I AM all things -

I AM - And for this thou art -

Awaken! Awaken - and be ye as one come alive!

Ye deaf and blind - Hear ye and see ye - And ye shall be brought out of bondage - So be it and Selah -

I AM -

Sister Thedra of the Emerald Cross

Sarah speaking -

Beloved children I come unto thee for the purpose of bringing thee home -

I am thy Mother eternal - And. I am the fortune of thy MALE PARENT GOD - Ye are because we <u>are</u> - Ye have been given form and being because we are -

Ye are because we Are - Because we called thee forth -

Ye are now called out from darkness - from all thy bondages - And we offer unto thee thy freedom from all bondage - as thy inheritance willed unto thee from the beginning - Blest are they which receive it this day -

I now speak unto my children as I have not spoken from the beginning - For it is now finished - When ye shall now do with the dark path which ye have chosen - Ye shall go out from me no more - Ye shall walk with me and talk with me - Ye shall know thyself and forget not that ye are ONE with me -

And ye shall have no need for the trapping of darkness - Ye shall have no need for all that which has bound thee within the dragons den.

I say ye are bound within the dragons den - And ye know not by what ye are bound -

Blest are they which are unbound - I say unto thee my children - When ye are of a mind to learn - When ye are so willed to accept thy inheritance in full ye shall have a host of light workers rush to thy side which shall give unto thee a hand -

And ye shall not want - Neither shall ye weary in well doing -

Blest are they which do turn unto me - for I shall give unto them that which is theirs by divine right - I am with thee and I shall bless thee as I have waited to bless thee -

I say my children - I have waited long for this day when ye should turn thy face homeward - and when ye might receive that which was willed unto thee in the beginning - Be ye as ones which can accept it -

By the Grace of thy Father-Mother shall ye return -

Be ye at Peace and Poise and I shall abide with thee -

I am thy eternal Mother Sarah -

Posite-Posa shall speak unto thee later -

Sister Thedra of the Emerald Cross

Sananda speaking -

My beloved children - I come unto thee as one of the Father sent - I come that ye may be blest as I have been blest - I give unto thee my love and my hand - I give unto thee of myself that ye may know as I know - I come that where I go ye may go also -

Be ye blest of me and by me - And give unto me thy hand and I shall lead thee into the place wherein ye shall stand before the great white altar and receive thy freedom - wherein ye shall stand face to face with me -

I come that ye may awaken from thy dream state and that ye may come alive and that ye may be forever free -

I say many know not that I am within the earth - Yet ye know me - And ye have walked with me and talked with me and ye know that I AM -

Now ye shall give unto them this word - And they shall bear witness of these my words unto thee and no man shall call me a liar - For I say that which the Father would have me say - And I bear witness of Him And none shall cut me off or close the door against me -

I say woe unto them which bear false witness against me or my prophets - Now when it is come that they bear false witness against me or my prophets the law shall be set against them and it shall deal justly and promptly -

I say it is no respecter of persons - And it is the law that anyone which-so-ever does place themselves greater than the law is forced to face his own folly par for par shall he be meted out his due -

I say he shall be unto himself judge and he shall be brot face to face with his own self - He shall be brought to justice - I have said a lesson learned is a lesson learned - So be it and Selah -

Bring thy heart and thy hand unto this altar - Give of thyself that others might have light - Be ye a living example of the initiate and let thy light so shine that they see it and follow it - Blest shall ye be - I am thy Brother and thy Sibor - Sananda - Son of God -

Sister Thedra of the Emerald Cross

Blest are they which come unto this altar in the name of the Father Son and Holy Ghost - Amen - So be it -

I come that ye may have light - I come that ye may be brot out of bondage - I come that ye may return unto thy abiding place - I am come that ye may know as I know - I am come that ye may be even as I AM.

And I am One with the Father-Mother God - I AM - And I know myself to be -

I have not separated myself from them - I am One with them and I AM - for that part not of a mind to separate myself from them - I go not out from them - Neither do I take upon myself a body of flesh substance. I am eternally a virgin - I create not - Neither am I created - I AM - have been and always shall be -

I was before Abraham was and I shall be when all the galaxies shall pass from their spheres -

I AM - And I am nameless - I AM formless - I AM soundless - Yet I AM all these things without me there would be No-thing - I AM that I AM - Ye name it and that I AM -

I come not - Neither do I go - I AM ever present - I AM the beginning and the end - Yet I have no beginning and I have no end - I am neither male or female - I am neither black or white -

I am not confined to any sphere - Neither am I confined unto any octave - Any part of any system - no galaxy - No place contains me - No part binds me - I AM freedom - I AM boundless -

I AM neither great - nor small - I AM all that which is REAL - I AM - I AM - And ever shall be -

I AM because I AM and none shall limit me by naming me - Yet I am called by many names - NO man knows me - for I AM the unknown. The unknown which is UN-knowable - I AM the Alpha and Omega - I go within - I go without - I am within - I AM without - Yet I go not Neither do I come - I AM -

I give not - Neither do I take - I need not for I AM all things - I AM. And for this thou art - Awaken! Awaken - and be ye as one come alive!

Ye deaf and blind - Hear ye and see ye - And ye shall be brought out of bondage - So be it and Selah - I AM -

Sister Thedra of the Emerald Cross

TRANSMUTATION

Sanat Kumara speaking - On the subject of Transmutation -

Ye have recorded that which I have said and it is clearly written while not clearly understood - Nor shall it be by them which have not the mind of comprehension - I say it shall be revealed unto the initiate for this is a great part of the work of the initiate which chooses to go the Royal Road - And for this shall they which are yet in darkness wait - They shall prepare themself for such revelation -

I say all is according to law - And such laws shall not be subject to the poor in spirit - For they know not the responsibility of such knowledge -

I say they are un-responsible and they are not trust worthy - Sad that they be - Yet that shall come forth in due time - Ye shall be as ones mindful of thy responsibility and of the power which is given unto thee. Such is thy preparation -

And sad is he which betrays himself or his trust -

Blest is he which goes the Royal Road - (here was a pause of 1/2 hr.)

Speak of this not lightly - for ye have as yet not comprehended that which is spoken of herein - Be ye as one prepared for the greater revelation -

I am Sanat Kumara

Sister Thedra of the Emerald Cross

Solen speaking -

Beloved children - I have given unto thee being - I am thy Father-Mother God -

I am not conditioned by matter- Nor am I made - I am not of the earth - Nor am I of any part of thy own Solar System - I am not of the substance of earth -

I take not a flesh body - Yet I cause flesh to become manifested in all planets within thy Solar System -

I <u>cause</u> it to be made manifest - I speak and it is done - I am not dependent upon matter - I AM matter - I AM Spirit - I AM Alpha - Omega - I AM all these things from which matter come -

I AM thy Father-Mother God - from which ye went out - I AM thyself-born of flesh art thou - Born once of me - Many times of woman.

I say ye have been born once of me - Many times of woman -

Ye have passed thru the womb of woman many times in which ye have lost thy memory of me - Ye have forgotten thy Source - Ye have not remembered it - Ye have had it blanked from thee when ye chose the way of Lucifer - Ye gave thy consent that it be blanked from thee - Ye have forgotten even this -

My children ye have forfeited a great inheritance - Ye shall now claim it - It is thine by divine inheritance -

Ye shall not be given anything until ye are prepared to receive it - Ye shall now ponder these my words - And give unto thyself credit for being my Sons-daughters

And ye shall step forth in all thy radiance and claim thy Sonship which is thine -

I say ye shall step forth and claim thy inheritance - I have willed unto thee from the beginning - And ye shall be born again of me - Ye shall step forth as one glorified of me and by me - For ye shall not die. Ye shall not taste of death - Ye shall be given a new body of light substance - Ye shall transmute all that which ye have misused within the realms of darkness - Ye shall be even as a God within thy own right.- For I have willed it so -

Ye shall be one with me and ye shall be as one qualified to give unto THEM that which ye have received - For I say as ye receive so shall ye give unto them which follow thee -

I say unto thee my children - Many shall come unto thee which are athirst and weary of their way - I say ye shall give unto them that which is given unto thee for them - So be it and Selah -

I am revealed unto thee that ye may come home unto thy abiding place - I am thy Father Solen - Aum Solen -

Sister Thedra of the Emerald Cross

Bor speaking -

Beloved of my being - Ye shall be as one which has my hand upon thee and ye shall be led into the place wherein I am -

I say we are within the place wherein we are in council for the good of all mankind - Not for the good of a few but for the good of all mankind - Wherein there are many which await thy coming -

Ye are as one which has waited and thy waiting shall end - So be it and Selah -

Be ye as one which has gone the long way and I say ye shall be as one which has gone this way for the last time -

Ye shall not be at the end of the coronation - Ye shall be at the ALTAR - Ye shall sit at the right hand of him which shall give unto thee thy new part and ye shall be blest of him and by him and ye shall be glad - So be it and Selah -

Be ye as one prepared - for one shall come unto thee and he shall give unto thee that for which ye have waited -

Blest shall ye be - Blest shall they be which come unto this altar -

Blest are they which speak with God the Father - Blest shall they be -

Be ye blest of me and of my presence -

I am thy brother Bor -

Sister Thedra of the Emerald Cross

Sarnica speaking -

Son of God am I - I come unto thee that ye may have light - I bring unto thee one from out the inner temple wherein the Father abides - Wherein there is only love - wisdom and TRUTH - wherein all things are known -

I say unto thee ye are on the verge of great discoveries - Blest are they which come into the place wherein all things are known -

Blest are they which do seek the light -

Blest are they which are brought out of bondage -

Be ye blest of me and of the one which I bring - for he has not yet spoken unto them - He has spoken unto thee when ye were in the High Andes - And great was thy love for him - Receive him now and be ye as his hand made manifest unto them - for he has much to give -

I say he shall give unto them which do receive him MUCH - He has received his Sonship and his inheritance in full - He has returned unto his abiding place -

Blest be ye of my presence for I come unto thee from out the Fathers realm that they may be blest of me through thee - And so shall they be blest -

Ye shall now say unto them as I would say and in my name that - When they have given unto themself credit for being a Son of God - and walk in the way set before them they shall be as ones given the necessary help -

They shall be brought into the place which is prepared for them wherein they shall be prepared for a new part which shall be given unto them to do - They shall be as ones responsible for all that which they do - And say - They shall be responsible for every thought - every turn of their hand shall be weighed in the balance -

For all the energy with which ye work is of God the Father and it is either used for to glorify Him or to torment thee - I say ye either Bless thyself or torment thyself with the energy which is portioned out unto thee -

Ye have free will to choose that which ye do - Yet ye are as ones responsible for that action which sets the law into motion -

I am now prepared to step forth and to aid thee in thy search - Yet in this new dispensation it has been made easier and safer for the initiate. For it is now come when many shall walk among thee for the purpose of giving unto thee assistance -

They shall not give unto thee naught before ye have prepared thyself for to receive it - They shell withhold all their priceless pearls with wisdom until ye have reached the age of maturity and understanding and are found trust worthy -

Blest are they which are found trust worthy - Blest indeed are they. While ye are found wanting ye are as ones blind - Ye are deaf - Yet when ye are found trust worthy of all the treasure house of knowledge ye shall be as one touched - Ye shall be quickened - And ye shall be as one come alive and ye shall Know and Know that ye Know -

Ye shall be sibored in the hours of thy sleep - And when ye have been so prepared ye shall be given a portion and ye shall step from thy old body of earthly substance into thy lighter body and ye shall go out into the ether and ye shall see the wonder of the Fathers handiwork - Ye shall cry for joy of it -

Ye shall bless them which have aided thee in thy search - Ye shall bless thy benefactors - Ye shall give thanks for being part of this plan - Ye shall rejoice with thy benefactors - Ye shall be as one prepared for the Greater Part -

Then and only then shall ye be free from all bondage - Shall ye drink of the Crystal Goblet of the substance of life - the liquid light which shall be brought from out the heart of God the Father and placed within the hand of one of His Sons which has likewise drunken from the goblet -

Beloved which do read this portion - Hear ye me - I say ye shall not be misled - I have said many times unto this my recorder that one shall come into thee which shall hold within his hand a crystal goblet beautiful beyond description and he shall offer it unto thee -

I say ye shall ask to drink -

I say unto thee my beloved children - Drink deeply - And ye shall not die -

Praise His name - Soler Aur Solen -

Sarnica Son of God - Am I - Be ye blest this day -

Sister Thedra of the Emerald Cross

Sananda speaking -

Beloved of my being - One which has come unto this altar alone have ye come - Yet I say ye are Not alone - For I am with thee - I am near unto thee - I shall not forsake thee for I have given unto thee this part - I have prepared thee - I have given unto thee of myself that ye may be prepared for thy new part -

I say ye shall walk among them as one made new - As one made whole - As one glorified of God the Father - So be it and Selah - I am one with the Father which has sent me and I say ye are as one which shall be brought out from the place wherein ye are as one prepared for the Greater Part - So be it and Selah -

Now will it not be for the good of all mankind that ye be brought into the place wherein I am and I say ye shall being one with thee which is yet within the world of men - He has gone out from the place wherein ye are and he has gone within his own place of another which he has chosen for himself - And he has chosen for himself that which he shall do -

And he has but to be reminded of his benefactors and he shall be reminded and he shall have his memory restored unto him and he shall be as one come alive and he shall be as one reminded of his Source of being and he shall be glad for his remembering - So be it and Selah -

Now say unto them which have come in that they shall have upon themself the responsibility of their own preparation - And for this have they been given the law governing their preparation - For it is now come when they which are to come shall walk among thee to seek out the ones which are prepared - And I say sad shall they be which is found wanting I am now going to speak unto thee on the subject of waiting -

Be ye as ones prepared for this day - And ye shall be glad - for ye which do wait shall be found wanting - Ye shall be caught up short of thy course - I say wait and ye shall be found wanting - And ye shall be caught up short of thy course -

Poor in spirit is he which waits - Now ye shall give much thought unto these my words - Ponder them long and ask that ye may be as one prepared -

And yet I say ye shall do thy part and ye shall be greatly rewarded. I say ye shall be rewarded - And too I say we do stand ready to give unto thee as ye are prepared to receive -

So be it our part to prepare thee after ye have done thy part -

So be it we do not betray ourself or our trust -

Be ye blest of me and of my presence -

I am thy Sibor and thy brother - Sananda - Son of God -

Sister Thedra of the Emerald Cross

Bor speaking -

Beloved of my being -

Blest art thou - Blest have ye been - Ye now have been prepared for the next step - Ye now have been brought before the great white altar - Ye have now seen with thy own eyes that which they shall see when come they which are privileged such - I say ye have stood upon holy soil - Ye have seen with thy own eyes that which is and shall be -

I say is has been and shall remain for them which follow thee – I say ye are not the first to come and ye shall not be the last -

Lose not the memory of this day - for blest shall ye be -

I say ye have been blest and ye shall now bring with thee thy physical body and ye shall bring with thee one other and ye shall be as one prepared to stay within this place for a period of time and ye shall be as one prepared for a part which shall be given thee to do -

Blest are they which do come into this altar - I say ye shall be true unto thyself and keep for thyself that which is for thee and give unto them that which is for them - And ye shall have for them abundance - Yet ye shall break no law. Ye shall bless them as ye have been blest and they shall be unto thee that which shall be unto thee my hand and my foot - They shall bless thee in turn -

I am with thee yet they shall do thy bounties and they shall be thy helpers - They shall be of service unto thee and they shall be unto the other hand with joy and thanksgiving shall they serve -

I am thy Sibor and thy brother - Bor

Sister Thedra of the Emerald Cross

Sanat Kumara speaking- unto thee of understanding-- Ye shall be as one prepared for the "GREATER PART"-- and ye shall say unto them in my name- and as I would say- that "THERE ARE NONE SO FOOLISH AS THE ONE WHICH THINKS HIMSELF WISE-- AND NONE SO SAD AS THE ONE WHICH BETRAYS HIMSELF"---

Now I say ye shall be of a mind to learn that which has been given unto thee-- And when this is learned ye shall be led into a new field of learning-- Ye shall receive great and wonderous revelations of the NEW AGE--

It is now come when new laws shall be revealed unto them which have been true unto themself and have learned the lessons well---

I say ye are not alone- nor shall ye walk alone- for ye shall be as ones which have my hand upon thee - and ye shall be as ones prepared for that which shall be given into thee to do -- ye shall be as ones prepared for the next step---

There is no other ETERNITY - other than this HOUR- it is OMNIPRESENT and this DAY is the only DAY ye shall ever know! for there are NO TOMORROWS- and YESTERDAY exists only in thy MEMORY---

Be ye as one which can apply thyself THIS DAY unto thee- and ye shall do well to study the law WELL- and to PONDER upon that which has been written---

I say ye shall determine this day thy course--and pity are they which are turned aside- for they shall begin anew---- BLEST are they which do attain---

Be ye as ones mindful of thy benefactors and ye shall draw them near unto thee and ye shall be glad for them-- I am come that ye may be brought out of bondage and ye shall be blest of me and by me-- Be ye alert for one shall walk in thy midst unknown unto thee-- When they have passed thy way ye shall wonder at thy slowness---

Be ye as one which can see beyond the mask- beyond appearance- for it shall be revealed unto thee one has walked in thy midst and masked shall he be---

I say be ye not deceived by appearance- for he shall wear a mask- not of paper- but of flesh-- see him for that which he is - and be ye not concerned with his appearance- for he comes from afar- with feet sore and weary- and ye shall give unto him food when it is come- and ye shall bless him- and let him go in peace---

Be ye blest by him and of him---

I am Sanat Kumara---

Sister Thedra of the Emerald Cross

Sananda speaking -

Be Loved of my being - Be ye blest of me and by me and I come that ye may be blest - I come that ye may have great light - I give unto thee one law this day and it is:

Be ye at peace within thyself - Follow in the way I set before thee and give unto thyself credit for being a Son of God - And bother not for the trivialities which beset thee - Ye have within thy hand the key unto the Kingdom and ye know it not -

Be ye as one at peace with thy soul and ye shall bless thyself - I can but point the way and set thy feet upon the path and when ye have been shown the way ye alone can walk in it - Blest are they which walk therein -

While ye are within the world of man ye see not the plan - Ye know not the fullness thereof - Yet ye are as ones which have a part which is necessary unto the whole - Be ye as ones prepared to pick up thy cross and follow me and I shall lead thee into the way which is new and strange unto thee and ye shall be as one which has earned thy passport into strange and new places - Many things shall be revealed unto thee and ye shall be glad -

I am one sent of God that ye may be found and brought in and that ye might be prepared and ye shall do that which is necessary to prepare thyself for that which is to be done and ye shall be as one joyful of heart and glad for all thy trials and temptations -

I say ye shall overcome all things and ye shall arise above the way of the uninitiated - Ye shall seek thy freedom from bondage - Ye shall WORK for thy freedom - Ye shall SEEK it from the Source - Ye shall go into the secret place and examine thyself and find that which is thy torment and cleanse it from thee and remember it no more - Turn from it after ye have transmuted it and ye shall remember it no more - Give it no lodging place - And give it no power over thee -

I say thy own discomforts are as nothing compared to the torment of one consumed of his wonton - I say be ye of a mind to learn - And I shall give unto thee greater things - I give not the pearls of great price unto babes which know not their worth - I am with thee unto the end -

I am thy Sibor and thy brother - Sananda - Son of God -

Sister Thedra of the Emerald Cross

Sanat Kumara speaking -

Be ye blest of me and by me - For I come that ye may be blest - Ye shall give unto them this word that them may know that which I say unto thee - They shall bear witness of these my words and they shall have within them the comprehension of that which is said -

Now for the first time I say unto thee - Ye have given of thyself that they might receive that which is given unto thee and they have as yet not received NAUGHT else than through thy grace and they are not mindful of thee - I say they are not mindful of thee - They are not given unto thoughtfulness and they are given unto the pettishness which besets them. They are as ones filled with little things - They have not forsaken them -

They are as yet not prepared for the next step - I say they give unto themself credit for being wise - They carry their weapons of defense as they go in and out - I say they come in on the defensive - they go out on the defensive –

They are as ones ready to defend themself and that which they have brought into the temple with them - They leave not their smallness nor their pettishness behind - They ask of themself counsel - They give unto themself credit for being wise - I say they have a way to go - Be ye as one which has my hand upon thee and ye shall not be deterred from thy way nor shall ye stumble -

I say ye shall stumble not - I say we are mindful of thee - We have not found thee wanting - We are not as one which forsake our own - Be ye of good countenance - And now ye shall be as one which has thy hand in mine and I shall lead thee and I shall give unto thee that for which ye have waited -

Now ye shall give unto them this part individually and they shall ponder it and they shall not make of me a fool nor shall they call me a liar - I am not blind - Nor do I betray myself - I see - I hear - There are no doors closed against me - Yet I enter not into the places wherein they turn against me -

I say when they turn against me I enter not -

Be ye as ones which have the mind to comprehend these my words and ye shall learn that which is said in secret shall be revealed openly - There are no secrets - Only thy own un-knowing -- Fashion for thyself the garment ye shall wear tomorrow - Fashion for thyself this day thy dwelling place tomorrow - And ye shall be the creator of each and every garment and each and every dwelling place -

Be ye either true or traitor - I say be ye true unto thyself and give unto thyself credit for being a Son of God and walk in the way set before thee - Ask of no man his opinion - Keep thy own counsel and be ye as one which has within thy hand the key -

Ye have but to turn it - It is clearly written and recorded within the laws herein recorded for all which do have eyes to see - Be ye as one which can see - Be ye not blinded by that which would hold thee fast - And that which would bind thee in the world of darkness - I am come unto thee that ye may be blest and when ye accept me ye accept my ambassador - my messenger in my name - And I have spoken and ye have heard me - I am and I know myself to be Son of God So be it - Amen and Selah -

Sister Thedra of the Emerald Cross

Sanat Kumara Speaking

Blest be ye this day- Thy eyes shall behold the glory of God- Praise ye His Holy name- Sing ye the songs Oh ye- all the nations of the Earth- Lift up thy eyes- See ye the glory of the heavens- Look unto the heaven for thy salvation - for it lies not in the Earth for ye have desecrated her and all that ye have created within her have ye created like unto the whore- ye have created like unto the unjust and the foolish-.

Ye have builded temples of stone and mortar- ye have colored them with the blood of Saints- ye have martyred thy Saints and named thy temples for them- ye have gone the long way to give unto thyself credit for being wise-.

Oh ye fools- ye babble of thy knowledge- of thy wealth and of thy love and of thy mercy- ye fools- I say this is the day of accounting when ye shall be caught up short of thy course- Ye shall be found wanting- Ye shall be brought face to face with thy foolishness-.

Now it is recorded and wisely so that there are none so sad as the one which betrays himself or his trust- Now it is come that ye shall reap what ye have sown and reap ye shall- I say ye shall reap as ye have sown and ye shall be as one which has sown into the whirlwind-.

I am come that justice may prevail- I say justice shall prevail- the law shall be served in all lands- in all places of the Earth and in all the firmaments of the heavens shall it prevail-.

I say justice shall prevail in all the lands of the Earth and none shall escape the law and he which would try is the greatest of fools-.

I address myself to the fools which think themself wise- which do plunder the temples of God- which desecrate the written word- which try to besmirch the servants of God- the ones which do send forth thy youth into battle in the name of God- I say oh ye fools- heed these my words- ye shall be brought to justice- ye shall give an accounting of all thy ways- ye shall be unto thyself judge- ye shall gnash thy teeth with fear and trembling at the might Power of God which has sent thee out from Him-.

Ye shall fall on thy face and cry out in judgement- ye shall call for mercy- and ye shall find none- pity shall ye be-

I now speak unto my servants for I am come that ye may be spared the great and terrible day- I say unto thee be ye as ones prepared for that which shall come upon the Earth and they which are true unto themself and their trust shall be caught up with the Might Host- for it is near time when there shall be a new port which shall draw neither unto the Earth- whereupon shall be the Heavenly Host and they shall pass near unto the Earth and the ones which are prepared shall be gathered together and brought in as ones so prepared- and upon that port ye shall be as ones prepared for the great day- when each and every one shall be removed from the surface of the Earth-

I say ye which are the remnant shall be caught up with the host which has been referred to as the Royal Assembly and prepared for the task which shall be allotted unto thee- ye shall return unto the Earth as man ready to do that which shall be given unto thee to do- ye shall choose that which ye shall do and then ye shall be given instruction in thy part and returned fully qualified to do it- Such is wisdom- be ye at the altar tomorrow for further enlightenment-

I am thy Sibor and thy brother Sanat Kumara

Rec. by Thedra

Sarah speaking -

Sori Sori Sori - O my children praise the name of Solen- Give unto Him all the praise and the glory - forever and forever - Be ye blest of me and by me - I am thy Mother eternal and I shall be unto thee that which thy Father God would have me be and I shall be unto thee the breath which ye breathe -

I shall be unto thee the life which ye are - for from me have ye gone out - I say ye have had thy being in me - through me and with me - And ye have forgotten me - I say ye shall now remember me and return unto thy rightful estate and ye shall be glad for thy remembering -

Bless ye this day - And give thanks for all thy trials and temptations and rise with me - Soar with me - Come my children with me into the realm where peace abides - Rest thy weary head upon my breast -

Leave behind thy little worries - thy small and trivial cares - thy puny talk and thy words which are sent into the eth so heedlessly - with no thought of that which they bring back unto thee -

Be ye as ones which can comprehend that which I say unto thee and I shall draw thee neigh unto me and I shall cause thee to hear my voice and I shall speak unto thee in the hours of thy sleep and I shall cause thee to be quickened and thy memory shall be returned unto thee - And for this have ye waited -

Blest are they which do receive their memory - I come that ye may have it so - Be ye as ones which can go from this altar this day with my hand upon thee - Walk with me - Hear me Oh my children for I am near unto thee even as thy hand and foot - Give thanks and be glad - Give thought unto that which has been said unto thee - Let it not pass from thee so easily -

Be ye as ones which can comprehend the laws set down for thy own welfare - Fear not and be ye as ones responsible for thy own preparation for ye alone can come - None shall bring thee unprepared -

Cleanse thy heart - thy hand and be ye as ones prepared to receive him which shall come. He will not be deceived nor is he so foolish as to give unto the unprepared the pearl without price -

I say he shall give unto thee naught until ye have prepared thyself for to receive it - Be ye blest of him and ye shall be glad for thy preparations - So be it ye shall call out and ye shall be heard and answered - I am with thee unto the end - I am thy eternal Mother Sarah -

Sister Thedra of the Emerald Cross

DIVINE EXPLANATIONS

Part - I

The following explanations and definitions of terms used by Sananda (Jesus) and the various Sibors were given by Sananda through direct revelation, July 17, 1964. They are not alphabetical. These explanations should be read over and over.

- - - - - - - - - -

"My Beloved Sibors please give us plainly the definitions of the following words that there may be no error on our part." - Thedra.

THEMSELF? What is the explanation of your terminology of "Themself" - themselves? -

"I (Sananda) say unto thee mine beloved, they which would be unto thee a vessel, unto thee a sibor, unto thee teacher, are as ones enlightened of the Father, enlightened of the Father for the light is in them.

They know their parts well, they have their memory, they have mastered the elements, they can do all the things which I do and they take unto "themself" no credit for they have overcome self. They are self-less. Now I say unto them: them which work with thee are the Selfless ones. They ask <u>nothing</u> for "themself." Now while this is true they are as one.

They are within the great brotherhood of the Selfless Ones - the Ones clothed in white. They are as the Royal Assembly - and each unto his own, yet each for all and all for one. Now while in thy world, they (of thy world) are <u>selfish</u> and they are not for the whole - they ask for self and I speak of these as the selfish ones. I speak unto them in terms which they shall come to know and therein is wisdom.

I say that they shall be responsible for "themself" and as a world of me I say they shall be responsible for their society; they "themself" have created it. Now I speak unto thee mine beloved, I say ye shall be responsible for thyself. He shall be responsible for himself. They as a whole shall be responsible for that which they have created, while thou art responsible unto thyself for thine part - and not held accountable for theirs. Be it so."

BELEIS? "Mighty is the word and great the power thereof. I say unto thee this word carries with it the part of surrender. The word is the release of power - that which is sent forth by the one which asks of the Father His blessing. It is the surrender of the self - the complete surrender of the personal will and letting the Father's will be accomplished in all things through thee. "<u>So</u> <u>be</u> <u>it</u>" - it the accomplishment, the acceptance of the Father's plan."

1 SELAH? - "The word carries the Seal of Truth - meaning it is without error - no mistake - it is the verification of Truth - not subject to change.

SIBET? – "The Sibet is one which has offered or presented himself as a candidate for the greater learning and for the greater initiation and he comes as an empty vessel that he may be filled. So be it."

SIBOR? - "I am the Sibor of Sibors." - "The Sibor is one which has been illumined of God the Father. He has returned unto the Father purified. He has gone the Royal Road - which means he has overcome death. He has mastered the lower elements - he controls the elements. He can raise the dead - heal the sick - he can create like unto the Father <u>for</u> he has finished his course and won the victory and returned unto the Father the Victor. So be it."

"I am the Sibor of Sibors. I am the first born of Him which hast sent me. Sananda."

LEGIRONS? - "Beloved - I say unto thee: thy opinions and thy dogmas are not the least of these - neither thy creeds. Be it ever that these are great and heavy ones. Now let it be understood that a leg-iron is something which holds thee bound. It is something which holds thee, it keeps thee fast, wherein progress is not possible. Now that progress be made possible, ye shall cut away the legirons.

Knowest thou these bound by legirons? These are to be pitied, they drag them with them impeding their progress - and they are as ones bound! They are not free - are they? While they serve their sentence - they are as ones bound - they are bond-men - they are bound men - men bound. Now let me say I too am a "bondsman." I came that they may be free. I say I bring unto thee the law which thou shall obey - unto the letter - then I shall give unto thee that which I have kept for thee. Be ye as one prepared for that."

PREPARATION? Now - preparation - what do you mean by "preparation?" "This my beloved is the part which they shall do - the part of preparation is: cleaning thyself of all the opinions, indoctrinations of man. The cup must be emptied. This is thy part, the becoming the "'little child" unopinionated, unscathed and unmarred with or by their doctrines, creeds, and crafts.

I say the child is un-indoctrinated and un-opinonated and is the virgin mind – (yet it does not remain so, long in this world). While the little child represents the empty cup - the empty vessel, the Virgin Spirit, it is given unto the child to be one which has come from other realms and to have been in many embodiments, many times: yet the symbol of virginity. Wherein is it said there are none innocent among thee?

WHEREIN I AM? - "Now while thou art yet within the world of men - I am within mine Father's realm, the place wherein there is no darkness, wherein <u>ALL</u> things are known. I say wherein <u>ALL</u> things are known, wherein there is <u>No</u> mystery.

And too - I say when thou hast attained unto thy Royal Road, when thou hast become part of the Royal Assembly thou shall know as I - thou shall be as I - thou shall be brought into the place wherein I am, for I say unto thee this is attainment. This is the day of Attainment, the day of "becoming," the day of thy salvation. Know ye that this is Mine day - the day for which thou hast waited? I say unto thee this is the day of fulfillment. This is Mine Day. Mine Day is come ---"

What is meant by "ALL THE LANDS OF THE EARTH?"- "This I mean, all the lands of the Earth. I have said it, I mean it as I have said it and there is no mystery of or to it."

ALL MANKIND? "This is Mine people - Mine children - Mine flock - Mine Church - Mine brethren - Mine congregation unto whom I shall minister. By Mine own hand shall they be fed and led. These have I came to find. Are not all <u>hu</u>-man beings considered "Man kind"? by thine own standards. Yet all men are not of me."

WHAT DO YOU MEAN - "WILL IT SO"? - "There is power in the "WILL" and the power which they use to create their own torment and confusion is misused energy. Yet they will this - they will it so. Now when ye will to serve me ye give unto me thy undivided attention, the whole heart - thy heart - thine ALL. Yet I say that they which doth attempt to serve me with one hand, and the dragon with the other - - has not willed to serve me. They are not of me - they are not of Mine flock. I say they are either with me or against me. I cannot accept the one hand while they reserve the other for the dragon. They are not wholeheartedly mine.

I make no compromises with the dragon. Mine shall come out from them and surrender unto me themself - their all - without reservation. This is willing it so - for they will the Father's will be done in them, through them, by them. They leave no energy that the dragon may use. They use all their energy to serve me. This is mine word unto thee."

WHAT IS DARKNESS? - "Thine Un-Knowing - thy darkness comes from the fall of man - which one was with God the Father perfect which didst have his memory blanked from him when he didst transgress."

MAYAS VEIL? - "The result of such unknowing - the darkness which man has brought upon himself. The part he has created for himself."

WHAT DOES IT MEAN TO <u>BETRAY</u> <u>ONES</u> <u>SELF</u>? - "This is the sad part for first the 'fall' came from his betrayal - and it hast resulted in the fall - in the veil of Maya - the "illusion" and in thy un-knowing - in thy own darkness."

WHAT OF BETRAYING "HIS OWN TRUST"? - "The plan is all inclusive and includes <u>all</u> - yet there are ones unaware of the "plan" - (and they are not as included in this temple as yet) - no personal reference unto the ones within this temple.

Now when one becomes aware of his part, he is given the law and it is provided for his own good - and he has the law clearly stated, plainly recorded, and he turns his face away - that he may hide from it. He puts his fingers into his ears that he may not hear it. He gives unto his benefactors the bitter cup and he goes his own willful way.

He has betrayed himself for he shall be caught up short of his course. When he has been given a chance - a "part" within the plan and he has committed himself, he has the responsibility given unto him for that "part" and should he be so foolish as to betray his trust he shall be like unto one which has thrown overboard his <u>own</u> life belt - poor foolish ones!"

WISDOM? - What is meant by the word "Wisdom?" - "Wisdom is that which is light, the knowledge of the law and its proper use. The right use of the law - and this Mine children is Mine part. I come that ye may BECOME wise! Wisdom is thy divine gift - not of man, for man of Earth is foolish indeed - and he is nothing save that which the Father has endowed him. All else is of the world of "illusion" which shall pass into nothingness in the Light which I Am."

WHAT IS THE "PEARL OF GREAT PRICE, THE PRICELESS PEARL." - "That which I offer thee - thy freedom, thy salvation from bondage - thine inheritance in full - Mine word which is not purchased with coin - not bought, neither is it sold. It is the wisdom of which I speak. Mine offer unto thee is without price - it is the 'pearl' - "Mine Pearl."

WHY ARE MIS-SPELLED AND GRAMMATICAL ERRORS USED IN THESE SCRIPTS? - "I am not a conformist. I am not concerned with the letters of man for I am He which has come that they be unbound by their fetters. I say unto them which desireth the letter - unto them the letter.

I say unto thee: be ye as ones free from such bondage. I stand ready to free thee from thy bondage. Unto thee I say - give unto the letter no thought. <u>Hear</u> what I <u>say</u> for I shall say it in many ways as becomes me and serves mine purpose. I say I am no stranger in thine midst. While they know me not, I know them. I see them bowing down before the Golden Calf - and they worship at the shrines which they have set up. (Their own standards of education.) They guild them and bring unto them burnt offerings - yet they close me out.

Be ye not so foolish. <u>Be</u> <u>ye</u> <u>not</u> <u>so</u> <u>foolish</u>! I am come that ye might have Light - Wisdom - Freedom which is the Father's will. While the letter changeth and passeth away - and the letter is not the law - the letter is of no consequence other than to cause thee to see the "Word." The word is the power which shall provoke thine mind into action and thy mind shall: be free from the letter. See what is meant within the Word, and let thine mind be staid on <u>me</u> - the Light, the Way - Truth and Wisdom."

"I am He which hast come - that ye be free: forever free. I am Sananda - Son of God. Once known as the Nazarine, He which was born of Mary, Ward of Joseph.

Recorded by Thedra

Part - 2

THE WHITE BROTHERHOOD AND THE EMERALD CROSS.

THE MANY QUESTIONS ABOUT THE WHITE BROTHERHOOD AND THE ORDER OF THE EMERALD CROSS MAY BE EXPLAINED IN A FEW SIMPLE WORDS.

ONE HAS TO EARN THE RIGHT TO BECOME A MEMBER - EITHER IN THIS LIFE OR OTHERS BEFORE OR AFTER---NONE ENTER UNPREPARED.

THE WHITE BROTHERHOOD - or - THE ROYAL ASSEMBLY is of the Realms of Light---not of Earth. The Ascended Masters have proven themself in the school of Earth (THE SCHOOL FOR GODS) who have trodden the path of INITIATION - overcome the trials and temptations of the mundane world - who have gained their freedom and ascended as the Lord Jesus Christ (Sananda). They have gone the ROYAL ROAD.

Knowing the path of the Initiate -- and its pitfalls -- and sorrow, they extend a hand in Fellowship - LOVE and WISDOM - NEVER depriving the candidate an opportunity to learn his lessons well -- for this is His salvation -- for this do they proffer their hand, NOT to do our part for us, but rather that we become strong and free by our own strength.

The Royal Assembly or the White Brotherhood have known all of the heart aches, the longing, crucifications, temptations and JOYS of the aspirant -- the candidate -- the Master -- the Sibor -- herein lies their strength, their understanding, their great love for us on the path.

Their love and understanding knows no bounds. They give help when necessary for our progress. They also withhold it wisely - should it deprive us of our lessons. The candidate on the path of initiation shall become self-responsible for all his actions -- all the energy allotted him throughout his whole EARTHLY existence - and make atonement for all his misused energy for therein is his salvation.

There is no one else which will ever make this atonement for us (the candidate) on the path of unfoldment. While the host of "WHITE BROTHERS" Brothers of LIGHT are ready to assist, the candidate shall (MUST) put forth every effort to overcome all the forces of darkness which would deter his progress and earn for himself his freedom from BONDAGE.

THE EMERALD CROSS

THE EMERALD CROSS - is a company - and order of beings who work within the Brotherhood of MAN - and the Fatherhood of God - for the food of all mankind --- And at the head of this group one known as MOTHER SARAH, the personification of love -- embodiment of all MOTHERS. That is: the LOVE of God made Manifest - in MOTHERS. The blessed Mother Sarah is the head of this Order of the Emerald Cross. And when one earns the Divine right and privileges to associate themselves with this Order, it is the joy of all the Orders - and Brothers of Light. I speak for the Order - for I am known as Merseda. As told to Sister Thedra of the Order of the Emerald Cross.

COMANCHE - which is the porter at the door - which doth keep out the unworthy, the unjust, the unclean. The Door Keeper - the one responsible for the Temple Gate.

BITTER CUP - that which you would not like to partake of - that which poisons thee - that which is not good that which torments thee - that which ye have given unto thy brother to torment him - which returns unto thee as a boomerang to torment thee - which ye shall receive multiplied - which has accumulated in its swift flight. I say prepare not for thyself the bitter cup for ye shall drink of the portion which thou doth prepare for thy brother. Be ye not foolish - make it not bitter.

BLEST OF MINE BEING - I have given of Mine self that Mine beloved has being.

BLEST OF MINE PRESENCE - Have I not gone the long way. I have gone out from Mine place of abode that I might bring light unto the Earth that she might be lifted up - that the children thereof might be delivered of all bondage - that they might return unto the place from whence they went out. And have I not come unto thee many times that this be accomplished? Have I not done all which has been given unto me to do? Wherein have I failed thee? Have I not done all that I have come to do? - While it is not as yet finished, I shall not fail. My mission shall be finished are I return unto Mine abiding place. Shall I not be unto the true and shall I not return the Victor?

GAVE OF HIMSELF - Did I not give of Mine Self - hast thou? Have I not been true unto Mine trust? Have I asked aught for Myself? Have I not done that which I have promised? Have I not given Mine

All? Have I not come on a Sacrificial Mission? What more have I to give - other than myself.

PORE - The physical body - vehicle which thou dost use.

INITIATION - Thy preparation for the inner temple. Each step is an initiation. One step at a time - the overcoming of self - the world - the becoming that which I am.

COSMOS - That which is unseen throughout many universes by thy eyes. Great is the expanse of the Father's Kingdom and the total thereof is referred to as "throughout the Cosmos."

LORD'S STRANGE ACT - This I shall reveal in Mine own time.

WALK WHICH WAY THY CROWN TILTS NOT - as a Son of God. Do honor unto thy Father Mother God - and thou shall be as one which has the Royal Raiment upon thine shoulders - and ye shall wear it in honor and with dignity.

WHEN IT SAYS IT IS RECORDED - WHEREIN IS IT RECORDED? - In the secret place - in the eth - and within the inner temple - and wherein thou art are many things recorded - which I do speak of. Ye shall see these recordings when thou doth enter into the secret place of Mine abode, I say ye shall read the records wherein are written the records of all thy travels from the time ye left the Father Mother God until thine return unto him.

WHAT IS MICHAEL'S FLAMING SWORD? - "The "Sword of Truth and justice."

Recorded by Sister Thedra

UPON MY HOLY MT

Upon My Holy Mt. I stand - and I see them, as I look afar, they who carry "My Cross", and they which serve ME, and on the other hand, I see them who sit by the way, and they are the "laggards" and they ask for alms of My Servants! While they do not give alms unto the Servants, yet they ASK for themself!

I say: I see them as ones asleep, they have NO comprehension of ME or of MY work or of the CROSS I carry for their sake.

I say: I see them as Laggards - they are not Mindful of My Servants! and the load they carry!

While they cry "Lord! Lord!" they turn their head when I say unto them: "BE YE UNTO IN SERVANT MINDFUL, THAT HE HAS FOOD AND RAIMENT."

I SAY: They turn a deaf ear unto My Words, when I say unto them: "BE YE UNTO MY SERVANT HIS SERVANT, FOR HE SHALL BE FED AND CLOTHED."

Now I say unto all which have received of Me through My appointed Servants, they shall make restitution in some manner - for this do I now speak unto thee freely and frankly! For My day is come, and as ye are prepared so shall ye receive.

I say: AWAKEN! Ye laggards and ye sleepers and be ye up and about the Father's business, for I am come that ye may shake off thy lethargy and come unto Me, and I say the day of the Lord is come! and ye shall put away thy childish ways, and turn unto the greater part! For this do I now remind thee of thy own responsibility unto My Servants and again I say: "As ye receive, so shall ye give."

For greater are my gifts, and no man can compare his puny penny unto my gifts which I have for him when he is prepared and I say as ye prepare thyself, so shall ye receive - IT IS THE LAW.

And I say it is so, So be it and I have spoken!

And I shall speak again, and again! So be ye WISE and HEAR ME. I AM "THE WAY-SHOWER - and the ONE who KNOWS EVERY STEP OF THE WAY. I AM, Sananda, -

Recorded by Sister Thedra of the Emerald Cross

Who Among Thee?

Beloved of my being - Go ye into the world of men and proclaim My name unto them, say unto them: He is come in flesh, flesh of My flesh and bone of My bone, and give unto them these MY WORDS - and I shall be responsible for them.

Ye need not fear for thyself, for I AM with thee, I AM He, which has given unto thee being. I have created the Earth, and the fullness thereof, and I say unto thee I AM within the Earth as one in flesh, and of Earthly structure, of the material substance, yet I AM not bound by any substance.

I AM the Eternal Father - SOLEN AUM SOLEN - sent forth as My hand thrust forward, to find there Mine finger at the point where ye findeth thyself.

I have created around my divine thought form My atomic structure which thou hast seen, and called "CHILD", and I have wrapt that form about with the substance of flesh and bone.

I have been as one born of another THOUGHT-FORM, sent forth for the purpose of bringing this My flesh body forth at this time. I am not alone - for I create of Myself that I might be accompanied by My children, I beget them of my spoken word, I command them to "BE" and they BEcome - I BEgat them for the fulfillment of Myself.

And now I shall be filled, and I shall withdraw My thought from the form, and it shall go into its original nothingness - for from My own heart have I created the form - the thought have I formulated, and the BEING that I thought was brought - "SEE WHAT GOD THY FATHER HAS WROUGHT! Therein is "WISDOM"

WHO among thee created by My thought? In My IMAGE!

WHO among thee can see My plan?

WHO among thee know thyself?

WHO among thee have knowledge of ME of My love My power?

WHO??

Say I unto thee they know not from whence they came - whither they goest - I say, they are a SAD LOT!

And they are as ones asleep under the black hood, yet for this have I come as one WHOLE - I have taken unto myself the atomic structure of Earth-being. And I say I Am not of Earth - yet I shall walk as such, but the Earth substance shall not touch Me, for I shall not be touched by it.

I shall never lose My memory of Myself - nor shall I give unto another the power to blank the memory of Myself from Me, for I shall walk among them free from any Earthly contamination, any Earthly taint, for I shall remain pure, even as I created MYSELF!

For I AM HE, which was, ever shall be worlds without end!

So be it I shall be with thee for a time, then I shall depart from among them returning unto my original place wherein I have given unto them a place of abode.

I shall bring with me all mine host which hast accompanied ME and I shall give unto them the reward which I have for them. Let it be said that it shall be the GREATEST reward, be ye among mine hosts which shall return with me, and I shall be GLAD. Let it be so.

I AM, the KING OF KINGS - Be it so and Selah. I AM

Recorded by Sister Thedra

The Thought Immaculate

Beloved of my being: Was it not said unto thee in the beginning that I should sustain thee - that I should give unto thee that which ye have need of - and have I not filled thy cup to overflowing? Have I not remembered thee in the hours of thy trials and temptations? Have I not poured out My Spirit upon thee? Have I not kept thee for this day?

I say unto thee I AM WITH THEE, I cradle thee in the palm of MY hand, and therein ye shall abide. Be ye at peace and poise. I say unto thee My Child, I am not blind, and I weary not of My lot for I AM thy Mother, first, and last - and always shall be, from ME hast thou been given form, from ME hast thou gone out.

I say unto thee, I have nourished thee and brought thee forth from the thought immaculate unto this present moment.

I say unto thee My Child, from the thought immaculate have I nourished thee, and I have MOTHERED thee in love and wisdom, and I have watched thee mature and expand, and prepare thyself for thy return unto ME. PRAISE ye this day, and remember Me thy Mother, and thy Father which has spoken the WORD and the WORD became animated and thou didst become a living soul. IMMACULATE IN CONCEPTION.

Now ye shall return unto me in the fullness of my LOVE, and Mercy and ye shall stand before the altar of the Most High Living God, and receive from HIS own hands thy crown, and thy inheritance in full.

Now I say unto thee, be ye at peace and abide with in Me, and I in thee, and one in ALL, and ALL in ONE - there is no separation from ME - only in their belief, their imaging, and therein is the pity of it all! I say, sad are they which know Me not.

Be ye as one prepared to return unto Me this day and I shall receive thee with a glad heart, and a BIRTHDAY shall be CELEBRATED, and it shall be a glad day! Be ye as one made glad!

I AM thy Eternal Mother, Sarah.

Recorded by Sister Thedra of the Emerald Cross

My Cloak of Authority

Beloved Ones: On whose shoulders I place My Mantle - My Cloak of Authority: I say unto thee - I am now prepared to give unto thee without stint - and with the authority which has been endowed unto Me of My Father - Love and Wisdom - and with all My being I come into thee as thy Sibor, and as thy Older Brother, holding nothing in reserve for Myself, for all that I have is thine, and all that I am is thine. I ask of thee PROVE ME! and I shall not deprive thee of anything which shall profit thee.

Now my Beloved Ones: I ask of thee nothing except OBEDIENCE unto the law. Be ye true unto thyself and follow ye Me - and ask of thyself have I overcome the stumbling blocks? and if not make haste to get them out of thy own way, for none other can remove them, Be ye as one prepared for the greater part.

Bless thyself as ye would that I bless thee. Be ye as MY hand and MY foot made manifest unto them. I am thy Sibor and thy Brother Sananda.

Beloved Ones, on who's shoulders I place My Cloak of the Authority, My hand rests heavily upon thee, and I say unto thee, great is thy responsibility and GREATER thy reward, the ATTAINMENT. Glad ye shall be for all thy trials, all thy suffering. For I say unto thee it shall be as naught unto thee, it shall be as the stars in thy crown, and brilliant shall it be.

I say I am with thee and I know what it is to be in the realm of flesh wherein ye are bound thereby, let not thy vehicles burden thee down. Grieve not for them which leave theirs behind, for it is now come when many shall transmute them and take them with them into the Light realms. So be it and SELAH.

I have said this shall become common knowledge, and it is so, for there shall be much Light shed on these laws which have hitherto been hidden from thee.

I say that these laws shall be revealed unto the just and prudent, so be it and SELAH.

Fortune thyself to be found worthy - I Am with thee that it be so - So shall it be that I am with thee for the purpose of bringing thee out of bondage - I am NOT found wanting - neither do I betray my trust - I Am thy Sibor-Brother, and wayshower which has gone before thee to show thee the way. Follow ye Me.

I AM Sananda, Son of God -

Recorded by Sister Thedra of the Emerald Cross

Behold Me! Thy Lord, Arisen, Alive

I AM HE, which was cricified and ARISEN - BEHOLD ME! I AM COME, I come that ye too MAY ARISE as I, and be caught up with me this day, walk ye with me, and rejoice for it is now come when ye shall know me and be one with me.

I am glad it is come, for long have I waited this day. GLORY! GLORY! be the time - PEACE shall reign, and WISDOM be thine.

Look not afar, for I AM here! I AM HERE! The day is NOW! I walk among them and they know me not, yet, I shall give unto them a sign, and a testimony, and for them which have ears to hear, they shall hear, and to them which have eyes to see, they shall see, for I say unto thee MY Beloved, I have hidden My face from the unbelievers, and I have not revealed My hand, while I walk with the ones believing! And I say unto them that which they comprehend.

And I say, that I shall raise up fools in the last day, and I shall make of them WISE MEN. Yet the ONE which 'think' themselves wise, THEY shall be found wanting, and THEY shall cry out: "LORD! LORD! WHERE ART THOU, HAVE YE TURNED AGAINST US?" To then I shall say: "BEHOLD THE WORK OF THY HAND, AND BE YE JUDGED THEREBY, FOR I HAVE CALLED THEE FROM OUT THE DENS OF INIQUITY AND THOU HAST TURNED A DEAF EAR UNTO ME - NOW YE SHALL SEE THE FRUITS OF THY LABORS, AND YE SHALL LINGER A WHILE THAT YE TRANSMUTE ALL THY MISUSED ENERGY, AND THEN, YE SHALL CALL UNTO THE FATHER WITH THY WHOLE BEING, FOR FORGIVENESS, AND YE SHALL COME UNTO HIM WITH

A CONTRITE HEART, AND AS A LITTLE CHILD AND HE SHALL RECEIVE THEE UNTO HIMSELF."

BEHOLD ME! The lamb of God - slain because of them!!

BEHOLD ME! The Son of God ARISEN because of HIS MERCY!

BEHOLD ME! Thy Sibor come unto thee because of HIS great WISDOM and LOVE.

I Am Sananda -

Recorded by Sister Thedra of the Emerald Cross

Mind Stuff

From the River of Life, do I come unto thee: for I am the ONE which hast come through the river of life; and I have passed both ways. I now speak unto thee of Spirit: of perfection of BEING and I say unto thee that the perfection of which I speak, comes from the river of LIFE; that which is perfect, created by God the Father in its completeness/ its completion, and it was created so in the beginning and it was as nothing else! Each thing was a separate idea - IDEAL - OBJECT - and a pattern as a multitude of patterns within a great tapestry - woven into ONE whole - ONE COMPLETE design, not to be separated.

Now I say unto thee, my Beloved - they, the unknowing ones, who are the most unWISE - have torn the tapestry into fragments, and fight over them: this is within their own little puny consciousness or animal mind - NOT in the CHRIST consciousness; for there is no separation, no divisions, NO PARTS - NO difference, except in the WILL, and the goat-mind; that of the thinking-man and his will.

He has had many lives in the realm of darkness wherein he has brought about his OWN HELL! I say unto thee, My Beloved, Hell, exists ONLY, in the MIND of the lower regions of man's mind, for they have created it!

I say I know whereof I speak - for they fortune unto themself such mind-stuff as they call "hell" - and it is so, this I too know, for I AM one of the Elohein, and I am fortuned to see and to know - I know what goes on in the realm of MIND, both on the lower and the higher.

I sit at the council table of the Mighty Council of Sun Spa; I preside on the Board of the WA-AT-EA-WA, (which ye may translate for them) - and I say I am qualified of My Father to speak unto thee on the subject of "MIND" and its results, for this is but the beginning of MY Discourse on the subject.

I say unto thee, I shall say more as it is convenient; let it be for the good of all mankind - I now withdraw, and give unto thee a blessing, such as thou hast not yet received - count them well; three by threes and ye shall count them - for great shall they be! I Am thy Older Brother, and thy Sibor Berean.

Be ye as ONE with ME, for this have I come unto thee; that yet may know that which I have for thee and it is now come when I shall Sibor thee in the way of 'Mind' - have I not said I would say more on the subject - and is it not so? Let it be so.

I say unto thee MINE is that which is given unto thee of God the Father and it is thy inheritance from HIM - thy endowment - and fortuned unto thee by and of HIM.

Now let it be stated, that when they are feeble-minded, they are NOT so by HIM, nor, has HE willed it so! Neither has HE taken from them his gift of mind-stuff, they have fortuned such condition unto themself. And it is fortuned unto every man which cometh into the world to have free-will and when he uses it WELL, for the GLORY of GOD the Father, he is as one given greater mind capacity, greater gifts -

And he has been as one given his inheritance in full; yet when one betrays himself and uses his gifts for his selfish end, and for the sense-gratification and to give unto his fellows the bitter cup, he is one which betrays his trust himself - his fellows, and turns his face from his SOURCE: and he forfeits his gifts for a time, until he learns his bitter lesson, and he then is reinstated into the House of the Father - with full-honors, as a SON and a full-inheritor of the kingdom of God and then, may call himself a Son: and be it not robbery to call himself "God" for Truly, is it not so? For has he ever been LESS? For did the Father not make him so? And did he not forfeit his inheritance for self: Which he has fortuned unto SELF?

Yet let this be understood: that to become God, and to become One with God the Father is to Know THYSELF; which is God.

Now was it not said that in the beginning God created man in His image and is it not so? He, the Father, made Himself a living CREATURE and breathed upon it and it became a LIVING SOUL. So it is clearly written, that he BECAME a living SOUL and that "image" which the Father did fashion "IMAGE" became a living soul by the breath which the Father, did breathe forth into His image this LIVING CREATURE.

Now it is said this living creature did turn his face from the source of his being and he did forfeit his inheritance and some of his gifts were taken from him and he became self: the animal-self; which is the chemical-man or the hu-MAN, and he is the animated creature mindless, shall we say? Void of this mind of GOD which was endowed into him in the beginning -

Now we shall explain this further, at another - Let us say, this living creature goes into the world as a pore, (which we call "MAN") and he walks with God the Father, he serves Him as His Son, he remembers his source and he gives unto the Father credit for his BEING - he give unto HIM, the Father, credit, glory, and praise, and he walks upright as "MAN" - He glorifies the Father as the Father has glorified him.

And he is endowed with certain 'gifts' and he draws upon his inheritance as need be and he claims his right and his SONSHIP, which is lawful, and there is no limitation of a Son of God - for I say unto thee - the Mind of God the Father is fathomless and perfect - it is the omnipresent and omnipotent. I say it is fathomless and omnipresent!

Now I shall speak at length on this subject at a later hour. Blessings be upon thee this day - I AM Berean.

By my hand shall ye be blest this day - for I come that ye be blest of me, thy older Brother. Be ye as one prepared to receive ME. I AM he which has come unto thee to give unto thee the discourse on "Mind" and I say unto thee it is my part and it is my joy, for I am as one prepared for this part. For it is for My preparation that I am able to Sibor thee in this manner, for I know the law governing such matters.

Now when ye become efficient in the law ye shall sibor others, even as we, thy Sibors, have sibored thee. I say WHEN ye become efficient in the law ye shall sibor others, even as we thy Sibors have sibored thee. Then, ye have earned the right to call thyself Sibor/Teacher/Master; and by any other name which indicates MASTERY. Yet ye shall not deceive thyself nor shall ye boast of thy attainment, nor, shall ye flaunt thy learning before the unKNOWING ones.

Be ye as wise and silent as the Sphinx, for therein is HUMILITY, and humility is a subject which I shall speak on at a later time - so be ye as one prepared to receive it. There are none pure without humility and that is one of the steps of ATTAINMENT - be ye as one which has attained - let it be so.

Blest are they which have attained humility - be it so and let it be said that the greatest among thee are the humble, Be it so, BE IT SO and SELAH.

Be ye as one which hast attained this state, and ye shall be blest with all the virtue of love. I say deceive NOT thyself, for therein is the greatest of folly, I come that ye may know thyself - let it be so.

When I speak of 'mind' it is the part which is given unto thee of the Father - and thy free-will conditions that "Mind Stuff" which is endowed unto thee in its virgin purity - yet because of thy free will thou hast become lost in the world of darkness and the great maze of trees which has seemed unto thee as a great black forest!

Now I say, ye shall come out of the blackness of despair, for therein ye shall have thy memory restored unto thee, and then ye shall know no darkness and ye shall have all knowledge of thyself from the beginning - and ye shall have the law revealed unto thee, which governs all the planets, and the fullness of them. I say there shall be no mysteries unto thee, for this do I now come unto thee that it may be so - I say therein is wisdom and the law which is hidden shall be revealed unto thee.

Blest are they which do receive this freedom, and gift of the Father/Mother God. Let not thy preconceived opinions trip thee up; and come as one prepared to receive of the Father thy inheritance in full; Bring not a cup filled with thy own offal/ thy own corruption, and filth for therein is the pity - for I say it is thy leg-irons - cut them away and cast them aside and be ye as a little child - clean and empty - void of all thy contamination - cleanse out the OLD and cast it off.

Prepare thyself to put on the WEDDING GARMENT - for I say unto thee the Bridegroom cometh and make haste to meet him.

O, Blest is the Bride of the Bridegroom, for he shall claim her and great shall be their joy - so be it and SELAH. Berean.

* * * * *

Be Ye of One Mind

Beloved - Was it not said that one should be sent unto thee, and was it not done? Has it not been done? I say unto thee I have kept my word - yea, I have done greater, I have sent unto thee three, and are they not my servants? I say they are "My Servants" and they are brought for that

"My Work" that My work might be accomplished in this the last day - I do say unto thee "THE LAST DAY" THE DAY OF THE LORD! When one shall go forth MIGHTY and STRONG - and this one shall proclaim his Sonship/ His Godhood and He shall be as one of God - come unto the Earth from the Etherial, wherein there is no darkness, wherein is naught but LOVE - for this does HE come that there might be LOVE among thee.

I say unto thee let there be unity and I say that there is naught within HIM which is come - save LOVE - for LOVE containeth naught save itself and love is contained within itself - for this is the "ALPHA, AND THE OMEGA" for therein is ALL that has been - ALL that ever shall be - which shall endure.

ALL WISDOM, MERCY, JUSTICE, which is LOVE. I say unto thee - be ye as "ONE" this ONE COMMANDMENT do I give unto thee this day: this I say again! OH, ye Children, how many times have I said - "Be ye of one mind" and I have given unto thee from out my LOVE - from out My Store of Wisdom, one which I have sent forth unto thee - that 'this thing' may be accomplished - that this the Father's PLAN may be brought forth in the completion, and in its fullness.

I say unto thee - thy work but beginneth, and mighty shall it be! I have said that I shall bring forth My Servants from out among them and I shall make of them "WISE MEN" and I shall make of them prophets in their own right -

So be ye as ones prepared to bear witness of me and to bear testimony of these 'My Words' "My Works"! For this have I given unto thee this part - now I say unto thee I shall confound the "wise" and I shall justify the JUST, and I shall lift up the lowly and the humble, and

I shall give unto them authority and power over the elements - and I shall be unto them that which they have need of.

Now I say unto thee "MIGHT" is the word of Solen Aum Solen, speak it with reverence, as a HOLY BENEDICTION, keep it holy and immaculate and bless thyself with it by keeping it ever in thy heart - I AM with thee and I bless thee with MY BEING. I AM Sananda the Son of God.

Recorded by Sister Thedra of the Emerald Cross

One Mighty and Strong

Berean speaking unto thee: I say, Blessings be upon thee this day - go in peace and be at poise - and carry the Light unto them which know not that He, the Lord of Hosts is come - I say give unto them this my word that He, the Lord of Hosts, the "ONE MIGHTY AND STRONG" has come and He is within the Earth as flesh and bone: and He is as one made flesh that they may have Light more abundantly.

I say, that they may have LIGHT MORE ABUNDANTLY - So let it be. Be ye as my messenger unto them - give unto them as it is given unto thee for them - for I say unto them that they are walking in darkness and they know NOT the Great DIVINE PLAN which is NOW in operation - and he which THINKS himself wise is a traitor unto himself - for he shall be faced with his foolishness.

I say unto thee deceive not thyself - for I am in the place wherein there is no darkness and I see wherein is MUCH darkness and too, I say that ye are a sad lot for thy unknowing - Now ye shall be as ones blessed to be up and about the Father's business, and ye shall be as ones led into the place wherein ye shall be given the law governing the elements of the earth, and for that matter all law shall be revealed unto thee as ye are prepared for such revelation - which is given through the SONSHIP of God the Father - by VIRTUE of the SONSHIP - through thy preparation and thou alone art responsible for thy own preparation –

Yet as ye do prepare thyself, a legion of GODS servants shall come unto thy aid, and give unto thee assistance - each having a part to give unto thee - each a gift which shall be given as the time comes as ye are prepared to receive it.

Now I say unto thee which art my hands and my feet - that ye shall earn thy reward - for it is ever thus - for not ONE gift is added unto thine others before thou hast earned it - Let this be understood! THAT NOT ONE ACT, ONE DEED, ONE WORD, PASSES UNNOTICED, UNWEIGHED ON THE SCALES OF JUSTICE!

For justice weighs all thy acts, all thy words, deeds, in the scales of life - time - and I say that justice is the law of LOVE which includes all VIRTUE - all which is GOOD.

I say unto thee MY BRETHERN, be ye wise and learn this law, and be ye governed thereby and return unto thy abiding place even as ye went out from the Father - PURE - and ye shall be like unto HIM in perfection.

Bless the name of Solen Aum Solen - I AM His Son by His Grace. Be ye the same BLESSINGS, BLESSINGS, IN HIS NAME.

ADOMNI SHELOHEIM -

Berean

Recorded by Sister Thedra of the Emerald Cross

Remembrance
Selfless Service

This day I would speak unto thee of remembrance- it is for the gratitude and the service rendered that there is this remembrance. For the service are we remembered- do we remember them which have served yea, unto the giving up of the physical body- I say unto thee even unto the giving up of their physical vehicle- yet no life lost, for life is not lost but the vehicle- while I say these are remembered for their service rendered -

Let it be said that this service for which these* have given up their vehicles is not the service of the great Ones which have served for countless ages for the good of all, and to bring forth the great and divine plan- this is the <u>Selfless Service</u> of which I now speak- I say unto thee let thine service be for the good of all- <u>Selfless</u> Service-

Let it be for the good of the great and divine plan- which shall be brought forth through such selfless service as that which I speak of labor not for glory for I say unto thee thine labor shall be for naught which labor for glory- for this is not selfless service. Which is of no lasting value-

The lasting service which shall be remembered by Me is without the coin- the puny penny- it is the giving of the self- with joy- and therein is the reward - I have said that I shall reward them <u>openly</u> which serve Me joyfully- let it be thine to claim- I am with thee that the labor of thine hands bring forth fruit- and it shall be a great harvest, and ye shall partake of the abundance- this is Mine word unto thee this day-

I Am the Lord thy God

Sananda

Armistice Day

* The ones who have served their various countries.

Recorded by Thedra

... Thou Art Sustained
I Am

This day I say unto thee, be ye as ones blest of Me and by Me, for this do I say unto thee, see the hand of God move-- see and know that I Am- for I AM- and because of this thou art sustained for thou art one with Me-

For this do I say unto thee see, and know that I Am- for I am one with thee- and there is no separation one from another- bless thine self with the knowing. Know ye this: <u>that</u> <u>there</u> <u>is</u> <u>No</u> <u>Separation</u>-- for I Am and for that thou art- I am the Father- Mother- Son- I Am the one- the three- no part but the complete whole- see ye the which is complete- such is the holy trinity no divisions, no parts-

One whole and complete- it is the beginning the end within itself complete- as nothing else is desired- nothing to be desired- this is the fulfillment of all that is to be desired for it is thine return unto thine rightful estate, thine inheritance, thine own divinity wherein ye shall <u>know</u> as we thine Sibors know- wherein all thine illusions shall pass and only reality shall be- and wherein there is no illusion-

Such is truth- truth and light <u>is</u>: they are one in essence and they are synonymous, and there is no place wherein there is one where the other does not exist- I say they are one in essence and these make up all knowledge- which is truth/light- it varies not- for truth is: ever present- and passes not away it is called Law-

While the Law of which I speak varies not- changes not, it is little understood by the un-initiated- it is such as the mortal mind does not comprehend- yet the initiate puts off the mortal mind and takes upon himself the mantle of truth- he adores the light- he turns from the darkness- he abhors the way of darkness- he sees the hand of God move- and gives credit where credit is due-

He wavers not in his way of truth and justice for his only thought is of truth and justice for all people- <u>All</u> things at <u>All</u> times: he is a shining example unto all- he is the personification of love and mercy, he gives no quarter neither does he take- he is self-sufficient, for he knows that he knows- he is the one which is known as "the initiate" for by his fruits he is known- so shall ye recognize the initiate by his fruits--

Be ye blest this day

I Am the Lord thy God

Sananda

"He gives no quarter" Meaning: He holds firm to what he knows- he is not moved by the world opinions- ("goat mind")

Recorded by Thedra

I am Come

Be ye blest this day- for I say unto thee <u>this</u> is the day of the Lord thy God, and it shall come to pass that <u>they</u> shall come to know that "I Am come" for this do I cry from the mountain tops- I say unto "them" I Am Come- yet the populace hast not heard Me- for they have stopped their ears with their own fingers- while they know not that I am come I say unto "them" which have ears to hear- <u>see</u>, and <u>know</u> that I am come- and be ye blest-

I say unto "them" Arise! awaken from thine slumbers- and be ye prepared to follow Me- that ye might return unto Mine Father with Me be it as "they" will it, for none shall bring "them" against their own will- be ye glad this day is come, and be ye blest for the knowing that I am come- for it is so!

Let this day be for gladness and praise ye the name of Solen Aum Solen- unto Him all the praise and the glory forever and ever- I speak unto all which has an ear to hear: I say unto them: praise ye the name of Solen Aum Solen- unto Him all the glory, all the praise forever and forever- <u>give</u> of thine self that He might be glorified in the Earth and sing ye a song of joy- let thine <u>heart</u> <u>sing</u> for joy for "this is the day of the Lord"- when ye shall come to know that which hast been hidden from thee- shall ye not receive in like measure unto thine giving? I say it is the Law- so shall it ever be- no man shall stay the law neither shall it be changed by mans opinions or thinking- know ye then that the law is just and perfect in its action-

For I am one with the law of justice and I know so be it-

I Am the Lord thy God

Sananda

Mine beloved- it is now come when I shall give unto thee this word for them- while they know Me not- I say unto thee they shall come to know Me- for this do I speak unto thee that they might know Me- have I not waited long that I might speak unto them thusly- I am the one known as the Lord of Venus- so it is that I am, and for this have I been given the privilege and the honor of this office which I now hold- and for this do I have the authority to speak unto these which I hold so dear unto Mine heart-

I say unto thee these children of Earth are dear unto Mine Heart- for this reason have I guided and Sibored them- I have nourished the Earth and Her children long- while I am little known by them, I have watched them come and go in their wanderings- I have heard their supplications and lamentations, I have seen them bowed down in sorrow, I have watched them adorn themself with fine raiment and set up fine altars in the name of their false Gods- I have watched them as ones on parade- as they go in and out of the physical bodies and wander hither and yon forgetting each embodiment as they wander forth, knowing not whither they goeth neither whence they came-

For this do we have compassion upon them for it is now come when we the guardians of thine Solar System draweth nigh unto the ones which are of a mind to receive us and of us- for this do we choose thee Mine beloved one- for this do I speak unto thee- for long hast thou served in this office of Priestess and Sibor- let it be; for I say unto thee thine work hast but begun- for greater things than this shall ye do-

By Mine word shall ye be blest-

Now ye shall say unto them in Mine Name that there shall be a great awakening amongst all the people of all the Nations and they shall raise up and cry out for surcease from all their misery and suffering- they shall see the folly of the way of man and they shall seek the light and it shall not be denied- I say not one which seeks the light <u>with</u> <u>their</u> <u>whole</u> <u>being</u> shall be denied- I say to that they shall not be deceived for there is no deceit within the light- I speak unto thee from out the realm of light and I know where of I speak- I am not a discarnate spirit wandering in darkness- I am free from all bondage and I know wherein I am staid- let it be so with thee-

Now say unto them which ask of thee: I am the messenger of the ones which are known as the Sibors- the word meaning "ones enlightened of God the Father": Ones free from all bondage- wherein there is no guile- be it so we know ourself to be one with the Father Mother God- therefore One with thee Mine beloved- therefore there is oneness of spirit- no separation- be it such as binds us together as one family "Sons of God" are We and I tell thee of a surety thou art Divine in thine origin- for thou hast been brought forth from out the Father Mother God as ones perfect in the beginning- hear ye that which I say unto thee and give credence unto that which I say- I say unto thee realize thine divinity, and walk ye upright as Sons of God the Father- be ye as ones blest forever and rest ye in the knowing thou art never alone--

I am thine faithful servant and Sibor--

Beloved of Mine being-

I am nigh unto thee always

Sanat Kumara

Recorded by Thedra

The Asylum of the Solar System, S. K.

Most holy art thou oh, sons of God, be ye as ones blest, for it is Mine privilege to speak unto thee from out the inner temple wherein there is no darkness- I say unto thee- "wherein there is no darkness" So be it the darkness shall pass away and the light shall remain.

Now it is come when great shall be thine illumination and great thine service- so be it many shall come unto thee and they shall ask concerning the greater things and they too shall be as ones prepared for certain parts- for certain work- and they shall go forth as ones prepared for such as they shall be given to do-

There are many of the illumined ones which stand by to give unto thee assistance- and they ask naught of thee, only obedience unto the law- the service rendered, the plan fulfilled is their reward- the children of Earth little know of such devotion and service as these selfless ones know- fortune thine self the greater reward and be ye as ones forever blest-.

Bless thineself by thine selfless service- while it is given unto Me to serve the planetary system for long, I ask nothing more than its deliverance from bondage- the Earth is Mine part which concerns us most- for I say unto thee she the Earth hast been a wayward child- the asylum of the system and now it is come when she shall be cleansed and purified and brought forth as a shining orb- justified in her suffering, and all shall be made new- and great joy shall prevail- for this do we work without ceasing- let it be so with thee- let thine service be thine reward-

I bless thee this day--

I Am Sanat Kumara

Hold High Thine Own Banner

Beloved of Mine being- the time is come when the fields shall not yield up the supply sufficient to sustain the people and they shall cry out for food- they shall leave their battlefields that they might find food to sustain their bodies- many shall perish for lack of physical food-

Yet the ones which sit in high places shall declare war and sit in counsel for peace and they shall be as one which have the cross bones and the skeleton for their symbol- this is the banner which they serve under- while I say unto thee, ye shall carry high the banner of the cross and the crown- and ye shall know no want for I say unto thee ye shall be productive- and ye shall grow and be as ones blest- waste not thine time on the wanton ones- grieve not for them- hold high thine own banner and walk ye as "Sons of God"- arise this day and come ye into the fullness of thine estate for ye have but to claim it in the name of the Father Mother God- so shall it be a goodly fortune indeed- be ye as ones blest and I shall speak unto thee again and again for I have but begun-

I Am thine older Brother

Sanat Kumara

Recorded by Sister Thedra

To the Ones to Come

Beloved of Mine being- this day I would give unto thee of Mine strength, of Mine love- that ye might endure- yet ye shall draw forth from the source of thine being the substance which shall sustain thee- now I speak unto them which are come unto this altar- the time is come when each and every one shall come to know that this "Is the day of the Lord" and that He is come- while I say unto thee He is come-

I to say they shall come unto Him in the time which is allotted unto them- for has He not gone before thee to prepare a place- now let it be understood that the day of preparation shall pass and they which are unprepared shall be found wanting- for none enter into His place of abode unprepared- let this be remembered while it is yet time I speak unto the ones which shall come- they shall come in holy remembrance- and for the communication with Him which is the Lord thy God- they shall be as sibets- as candidates for the greater revelation- then they shall have the assistance and guidance necessary unto their initiation- forget not this is the path of initiation- and let it be remembered that there are none so sad as the ones which betray themself- I say unto thee they are the saddest of the lot- while I am the one known as the worthy Grand Master-

I say it is Mine duty to speak unto them of certain things which concerns them- first, <u>Love</u> <u>ye</u> <u>one</u> another- serve selflessly- and with joy- hear ye the words which is given unto them and be ye as ones prepared to give of thine self without reservation- unto them which have not the "word" neither the strength nor the desire to learn- yet ye shall be as ones blest to offer up thine self on their behalf- ye shall not in <u>any</u> <u>way</u> trespass upon their free will- neither shall ye bring them against their will- I say unto thee be ye as the candidate for the greater learning-

While much hast been given unto thee- there is yet more- close not thine ears- or thine hand- reach out that it might serve the greater plan- for this have I spoken that ye might be part of the greater and divine plan- let it be so--

I Am thine older brother and Sibor known as

The Most Worthy Grand Master

Recorded by Thedra

Sananda Speaks unto the Father

Most holy Father Mother God. I give unto thee all the praise- all the glory- I bring unto thee these thine children which have asked of Me, that they be delivered up- into thine keeping I give them- for this Mine part I am finished- I have come into their midst that they might come to know thee. O, Father I come unto them as thou hast sent Me, of Mine own free will I come- now I give of Mineself that they might come to know the joy which is given unto one which hast returned into thee-

Be it so Father that they all return unto thee with Me, for this is the time of fulfillment for these thine children- for this have I revealed Mineself unto them-

Now I say unto them: <u>hear ye that which I say unto Mine Father for He and I are one. I know Mineself to be one with Him</u>--

Glad am I that I am privileged to come unto them Father that they might be prepared to return unto thee with Me- I Am Glad! So be it Father that this is My part and I have accepted it in thine name and unto thine glory shall it be finished-

Be it so that they shall follow in Mine footsteps and go with Me where I go- let it be as thou hast willed it-

I Am Thine Son

Sananda

This Day Shall Bear Fruit

Behold the hand of God made manifest- see that which He shall do- see the manifestations of the word, for I say unto thee the word hast gone out from His mouth that this day shall bear fruit; new fruit such as thou hast not tasted of- let it be the fulfillment of all thine labors- for I say all thine labors shall be as one account- they shall be added up- and they shall be weighed in the balance and there shall be no lack- for I have said it shall be fulfilled- the end shall be a glorious triumph and ye shall stand as the victor- and triumphant shall ye return unto thine abiding place- I say ye shall return unto thine abiding place victorious and thine joy shall know no bounds- so shall it be a glad day-

I Am with thee this day

I Am Sananda

Recorded by Thedra

Love

This day I would speak unto thee of love- it is now come when ye shall come to know the meaning of "LOVE", for it thou art sustained- I say unto thee because of the love which we bear for thee art thou sustained- while We thine benefactors work without ceasing that the great and divine plan be brought to fulfillment thou dost weary of body-

Yet ye shall remember that thine body is but a fragment of thine own creation which shall change and change as the rainbow colors- While I say unto thee O, Mine beloved ones thou art not mortal flesh- thou art of light substance which shall not pass away, which shall not perish- neither is it bound by flesh- listen ye unto Mine words; for I say unto thee: "<u>thou art not mortal flesh</u>" thou art a threefold being- and ye shall not die- for thou art eternal beings- thou art beings of light substance which perish not- be ye as ones which <u>know</u> - know ye that I dwell with thee- that I am the Lord thy God- and I shall bless thee this day- ask of no man his opinion for I say unto thee man's opinions are such that they trip thee up- let thine feet be planted firmly upon the rock which I Am- for I Am the Son of God- sent that ye might return unto Him the Father with Me-

I AM

Sananda

The Father Speaks

Beloved of Mine being I speak unto thee out the fullness of Mine being- and words cannot express the fullness of Mine love- Mine being- for thee- for I say unto thee thou art of Me and by Me- for I am thine Father which hast brought thee forth from the beginning of thine existence as a personality- I say unto thee thou art Mine creation - for from Mine being hast thou come forth- let thine hands be Mine, thine mind be Mine- for I say unto thee thou art of Me and without thee I should not be whole- for without thee I should not be perfect- I am no less for sending thee forth-

I am no more for bringing thee home- yet Mine joy shall be created when ye return unto Me- there is great joy in the cosmos when a Son returns unto his abiding place and receives his inheritance- ye shall come to know for I say it is now come when thine bondage shall end- and ye shall return unto Me unscathed, unharmed- for this have I sent Mine Sons that ye might awaken unto thine identity- I say unto thee remember thine inheritance is greater than all the wealth of the Earth- yea that of the Solar System- for all I have is thine- be ye as Sons of

God thine Father- walk ye as such amongst thine fellow men and be ye as ones prepared to return unto Me- so be it there shall be great joy throughout the cosmos- so shall it be- as I have sent forth a fiat that it be so- so let it be-

I Am thine Father

Solen Aum Solen

Recorded by Thedra

Ye Shall Be Unveiled

Mine children rest in the knowing that thou art the Sons of God the Father- born of Him art thou- brought forth through His mercy by His grace- and because of His love shall ye be brought back unto thine abiding place-

Now it is written that ye shall come to know Him the Father as I know Him, yet it is given unto thee to be sorely oppressed- yet I tell thee thine oppression shall be as naught- for it shall pass and ye shall stand forth as the sentinels of light- the Sons of God which thou art- I say ye shall be unveiled and ye shall step forth as the Sons of God which thou art- let not the veil blind thee for I tell thee it is but the flesh which blinds thee- it is the veil of illusion, be ye not deceived- while I say unto thee the illusion shall pass and ye shall stand as the sentinels of light which thou art- thou hast been brought forth as such- while thou hast seen the flesh and called it "self" I tell thee it is the illusion- for the reality is that which is and shall ever be without end-

So be it the <u>endless</u>- for there is nothing which is <u>real</u> which shall pass- that which is endless changes as the Son, as the colors of the rainbow Scintilates as the colors of the borealis- and takes unto itself greater and grander forms- while the Sun is the Sun it never is less for its many rays which go out from it- hear ye that which I say unto thee and be ye of a mind to learn- for the forms of man changeth and changeth from one into another, and ever greater more perfect shall they become until thine eyes could not behold such perfection as that of the glorified man- I say unto thee: thine eyes could not look upon such perfection as the glorified man- so be it that thine eyes shall be made to see- for thine eyes shall be opened and thine mind quickened and ye shall behold Him in all His glory- So be it and Selah-

I have spoken and thou hast heard Me-

I Am Sananda

The Love We Bear

This day be ye reminded of the love which we bear for thee- for I say unto thee it is because and for that love which we bear that We stand by to give unto thee assistance, I tell thee of such love yet thou cannot comprehend the fullness of such while thou art looking amongst men- for no man knoweth such love of himself-

Yet such love <u>is</u> and shall ever be: for this do I say unto thee let thine service be selfless- selfless love brings selfless service- and selfless service the greater reward- the GREATER REWARD is thine INHERITANCE--

Such is Mine word unto thee this day- so be it I am the Lord thy God-

Sananda

Recorded by Thedra

The Father Speaks: Of His Son

Beloved children- the time is come when I have sent Mine Sons unto thee in great numbers, that ye be brought out of darkness- released from thine bondage- yet I say unto thee- thou hast not shaken off thine leg iron- thine opinions, thine preconceived ideas of Me thine Father which hast sent these Mine Sons to awaken thee- Now I say unto thee: these are Mine children- these are Mine Sons and Mine Daughters which I have sent forth that this Mine word might be made known to thee- I say unto thee these which I have sent into the world of man are Mine hands, Mine feet made manifest unto thee that ye might come to know thine origin, thine own identity- I say unto thee thou hast lost thine way- "The Word" hast been sealed up against the rebellious ones that it might not be pilfered and misused-

While I say unto thee, hear that which I say and keep "The Word" sacred and holy- be ye not so foolish as to adulterate it for it is but the greater part of foolishness- I say unto thee I am and I am thine Father eternal- I have brought thee forth: from out Mine mouth did I speak the word which hast given unto thee being.

Now ye shall be as ones prepared for thine return- I send Mine Son which I have chosen unto them which are prepared to receive Him- that

He might touch them and be made whole- I tell thee- ye shall be as one prepared, for He shall find thee by thine own light in the place wherein ye are- ye shall walk upright, honorable in His sight- forget not He sees thee for that which thou art- give not the bitter cup unto any man- hear ye that which he has to say unto thee for I have sent Him unto thee as Mine own Son, appointed by and of Me for this His part- this part is not new unto Him for He hast come many times as Mine hand made manifest unto thee- He is Mine hand, Mine foot, Mine voice- Hear ye Him and follow ye Him- for I say unto thee He is come that ye might be prepared to return unto Me with Him--

I say unto thee He Mine Son is the one which I have chosen from among the host which is come unto thee- that ye might awaken and return unto Me with Him; for He is the Lord of Lords, the Lord of Hosts- ye shall be as one blest to receive Him- I speak out this day that ye might come into the fullness of thine being- I am not finished,

I AM the Father- I AM the Mother- I AM the Son.

Solen Aum Solen

Recorded by Thedra

Christ Mass - 1965

Blest are they which remember Me sayeth the Lord thy God, blest are they which keep the law-- blest are they which go with Me for I am come that they which are prepared might return unto Mine Father with Me--.

This is the day of remembrance when they come to know that which hast been hidden from them- I say unto them which seek light- this is the age of light- the time of knowing- and all which are prepared shall come into the fullness of their being- for it is written that this is the time of the end and the time of the new beginning- the old shall pass away and the new shall be established so let it be as the Father hast willed it.

This is the day of putting off the old- taking up the new- and the old shall pass away as nothing, and be no more- the new order shall be established and all which are prepared shall dwell in the house of the Lord--.

I say unto these which are prepared- come ye out from among the hypocrites and the transgressors and let thine light shine that they might see it- be ye no part of their hypocrisy, their blasphemy-- ask of them naught except obedience unto the law- waste not thine time on them-- for I say unto thee it is thine part to obey the law and let thine own light shine that they might see it and be drawn unto it*.

Blest are they which seek truth and justice for they shall be justified by the law- wast it not said that justice shall prevail- for it is the will of Mine Father which hast sent Me-.

SO BE IT I AM COME THAT THERE BE LIGHT -

So be it I Am

Sananda

*Teach by example

Recorded by Sister Thedra

The Lords Compassion

Sanat Kumara speaking- Beloved of Mine being- it is with great compassion that we wait for them which are yet in bondage- yet they shall be as ones bound until they choose to come of their own will- I would say unto them: there is great and powerful ones which await to give thee assistance, when ye choose to accept it- they which are of a mind to accept such assistance shall be glad indeed.

For this do We the Sibors wait with longing in our heart, for we know such freedom as thou hast not remembered- while it is the law that ye be of a mind to receive and to accept that which We bring- I say, there is none so pitiful as the ones which reject us, that which We have for them- the Sibors draweth nigh unto the Earth that She might be lifted up- while it is the place of the laggards- there are many which have gone out from their abiding* place that they might be found and brought home- I say- some have foresworn their own freedom that others might be freed from bondage. While they have wandered under the cover of night**-others have followed after them that they might be awakened unto their divinity and brought back--.

I tell thee, they are divine in their origin, in their progression and therein is a great story***- the drama of the Earth and the Heavens are written therein--

I say unto thee: be ye as ones playing the greatest drama of all times. Know thine self to be participants within this great play and be ye as ones remembering that which ye do and have done--

Seek ye the light- ask and ye shall receive--

Be ye blest for the seeking- rest in the knowing the Lord thy God is come-

So be it I shall speak again and again--

I AM Sanat Kumara

Recorded by Thedra

*Orign/home

** darkness/unknowing- they too fell asleep-

*** "The Prodigal Son"

New Year! New Day!

Beloved ones- this day I would say unto thee the time is come for the sifting and the sorting- (the harvest) and this is the day for which ye have waited- the day of the end- the end time, when thine wandering shall be finished, completed, finished to be repeated no more--

Now while it is so- I tell thee ye shall prepare thine self for a new beginning- thine new part- what a glorious new part is prepared for thee, and what a glorious new day thou art beginning and what a bountiful harvest it shall be- let it be a time of rejoicing! look unto the mountain from whence cometh great strength and see the glory of that which lies before thee: let thine hearts rejoice for this day- be ye glad it is come- look unto the East see the sun cometh up from out the East- know ye that there is a plan far greater than man hast imaged- be ye as one and sing within thine heart songs of gladness- so let it go out unto all which are prepared to receive the new day for great shall be the light which shall flood the Earth and all which receive of it shall be made to rejoice. Let it be so with thee-.

Be ye at Peace and poise---

I AM the Lord thy God

Sananda

Ones to Come

Blessed are they which come unto this altar for they shall be given comprehension- I say: "they shall be given comprehension" let it be so- for this do I bring them- I say unto thee for <u>this</u> do I bring them that they might be given comprehension-

Now there are ones which shall come which have little comprehension, and <u>these</u> shall be as ones prepared for the next part which shall be given unto them- I say unto thee give them naught which would choke them- for they would but <u>choke</u>- the way is open, and the time is come when ye shall receive them and prepare them for the next step- yet some shall <u>not</u> step forth as ones able to walk forth under their own strength or by their own efforts: let not these ride thine back- for I say unto thee they shall put forth the effort and they shall be rewarded- So be it I have spoken and thou hast heard Me-

I Am Sananda

Recorded by Thedra

Christ Speaks

Sori, Sori - the Christ speaks unto thee this day, that which is Spirit sayeth unto thee - Behold that which is Spirit - that which is Eternal and which is pure - pure of its purity by divine endowment, of the Father's virtue made pure,

I say that Spirit is life - pure in its purity which is of God the Father, by His Virtue and by His Nature - Now ye shall be unto thyself true, and declare for thyself thy freedom from bondage - thy freedom from darkness and ye shall cleanse thyself of all preconceived concepts of the Father/Mother God, -Thy Source. For I say unto thee, man of Earth, ye have not conceived the fullness of HIM the Father, nor HIS handiworks, for he has been as one whose head is bound and he has enshrouded himself in a great mist, he is enmeshed as a fly enmeshed within the web of the spider.

He has been indoctrinated through the ages from the beginning of thy sojourn and he has gone in and out of the flesh as a wanderer in darkness, and he returns again and again to find himself entangled within the same web and he has played his part in the weaving - for not one stands alone in his enmeshed condition.

Yea, sad indeed - the mass is enmeshed as a fly! I say it is INDEED sad! For not any one stands alone for as a people dost thou go out, and as a people dost thou weave the "web of illusion."

And I say unto thee only thy own effort, thy own free will can free thee - for therein is thy freedom, and let it be for the good of all that ye seek thy own freedom - for therein is wisdom.

I say unto thee great and powerful are the ones now sent to bring thee TRUTH, LIGHT and LIFE - more fully shall ye live, greater shall be thy work and lighter thy way and great shall be thy reward.

I say unto thee ye shall be as one free from all thy dogmas and creeds, thy leg-irons, bondage - and ye shall be as ones free forever - Yet I say unto thee this day, ye shall will it so - So be it and SELAH. Now ye shall be as one prepared to receive the greatest revelation. Now in this day when ye have cast aside thy preconceived ideas of thy source, of thy God and of His Son, of thy own BEING - and of the universe about thee.

I say ye have been given false doctrines and ye have adulterated even them! Now I say unto thee, the time draweth nigh when ye shall go into the secret place of the Most High Living God, bare - bare - as a new-born babe - void of anything, save thy eternal SOUL, and it shall be clean - for none other shall enter therein.

Behold thyself, this day, as a CHILD of the MOST HIGH LIVING GOD - and be ye as one clean - come as a little child, void of all thy preconceived ideas, of all thy rituals and all thy creeds; and ask of HIM thy Father, thy freedom. When ye have asked as a little child in humbleness, and with a contrite heart HE shall have compassion on thee and HE shall accept thee as HIS own with LOVE and compassion and HE shall be unto thee the Father of love and mercy - So be it and SELAH.

I give of myself that this may be my gift unto thee this day - I am Sananda, the Nazerine, Son of God AM I, sent to show thee the way - follow ye Me, I AM the one gone before thee that the place be prepared for thee. It is done and I AM come that ye may return with Me - Let it be so - Sananda.

Recorded by my servant, my hand made manifest - she is one with Me - I AM the hand - I AM the mind - I AM the One sent of HIM, My Father that prophecy may be filled. She is my servant which I call Thedra, is thy benefactor, even as I AM hers. Remember this - as ye would that I remember thee.

I Would Speak Unto Thee of Devotion

Beloved Ones: This day I would speak unto thee of devotion, devotion unto the great and Mighty, Allwise Giver of Allgood and Glorious gifts. I say unto thee MIGHTY is HE, was and ever shall be!

I speak unto thee this day as one which has gone the Royal Road - and I am qualified to speak as thy Older Brother, for I am. Now let it be understood that when one is called out from among them and they have answered the call this sets 'them' apart from all others, from them which are yet in darkness.

Now when they answer the call they are as ones set apart, for this have they been called, and when they give of themself wholeheartedly with all their will, all their energies, they devote themself to the work at hand and they divide not themself, they give not of themself to the things of the world - neither do they run hither and yon seeking man's opinions, or favors; for I say, they MATTER NOT!

Now when they, the ones called out are so prepared for any part which is prepared for them, then they shall receive it, NOT until they are prepared for it, and wherein is it written, that as they are prepared so shall they receive? So be it and SELAH.

Now I say, they which are devoted unto the plan, and are found trustworthy shall be greatly rewarded, for they shall be as one which has "earned the right" to call themself "Teacher/Master/Sibor" or any other name - I say, by any other name they <u>earn</u> the right, which is their passport and they pass not through the portals of the temple of Light until they have proven themself worthy.

I say as they are prepared so shall they receive - So be it and SELAH. I say unto thee, be ye as one devoted unto thy calling - let NOTHING turn thee aside, and give unto the altar all thy energy, all thyself, all thy time, for this have I brought thee hence, for this have I commanded thee "FOLLOW YE ME" and I go not into the place of iniquity and I go not into the dens of thievery. I go not wandering. I say I Am alert unto my part, and I am about My Father's business and naught else. By my hand shall ye be staid while thou dost obey my commandments, yet, I say unto thee; I sibor not fools, for they are as the foolish, and they are not as yet prepared to receive that which I have kept for them. So be ye as wise as the serpent and silent as the sphinx. I am thy Sibor and thy Brother Sananda -

Recorded by Sister Thedra of the Emerald Cross

Judas, the EGO

Beloved of my being: by My hand do I bless thee this day - and let this be recorded for them which are of a mind to read that which I have commanded thee to write. When it is given unto one of mine to set himself up, he is then as one which has come down in thy history as "Judas" - let this be recorded also, Judas, is that which prompts man to betray himself, it is the 'ego' and not the Father which does these things, for it is not of the Father that they punish themself, for has He not sent a host unto them that they may know wherein they are staid?

Yet I say unto thee - the ego, Judas, is the betrayer, and it is the pity of it, for I say that when they do boast of their learning and of the revelation they are as foolish babes which know not that which they say, for I say unto thee - it is many a mile yet unto the end.

Yet I say beware, lest thy foot slip - be it a straight and narrow path, yet within that path are many pitfalls - yet too, I say I know them all and I say boast not of thy learning, for it is not yet revealed what manner of man thou art.

I say unto them, be ye as silent as the sphinx, and ye shall become wise! Listen not unto their bragging and their boastings, for I say they are as ones puffed-up, and too, I say they shall be brought low.

I too say: I bargain not with them, neither do I give unto them that which I have kept for them UNTIL they have grown unto the age of accountability and then I say unto thee they put away their boasting and their childishness, for it is not becoming a Son of GOD.

Now let this be understood - I DO NOT SIT IN THE SEAT OF JUDGMENT! Yet I know them for that which they are and too, I say, that there are many of the great ones among thee which are still in darkness and know not from whence they came nor whither they goest.

Yet I say, that they which do speak of the greater part and which have as yet not received such revelation are as prattling babes - and when this greater part is bestowed upon them they speak not of it - they walk in silence and in dignity, they speak not of their goodness, their virtues their good fortune, their good qualities - and they walk quietly among their fellow men doing service unto them asking of them naught, I say unto thee great is the law and powerful is it and it is given unto me to see them rushing hither and yon seeking of men their blessings, their favor and their recognition and their fortune. While I say unto thee PEACE AND POISE.

Be ye as the MIGHTY OAK - Be ye not uprooted by the breeze, yea, not even the winds shall uproot thee. I say be ye as the ROCK upon which I shall build my temple, upon which I HAVE builded it. Look not forward nor backward, yet rather watch thy footstep. Place it firmly within my footsteps and I shall lead thee safely through the shadows, I am with thee and I shall not forsake thee. I AM Sananda.

Recorded by Sister Thedra of the Emerald Cross

O, Mighty Sons of Israel

Mighty is the word! Praise ye this day and be glad it is come - praise ye the name of Solen Aum Solen.

Hear Me! Oh, ye children of Israel, for I am the voice of Israel! and I say unto thee: "Ye are the Children of Israel, and ye are the ones which I have gathered from out the multitudes!" I say: "From out the multitudes have I gathered thee!"

I speak unto thee as one knowing - I speak unto thee as one which has come to claim my own, harken unto me, o ye children, for I am come, I am come - make haste! and wait no more for signs and wonders! For I am in the Earth as one of flesh and bone!

And I say unto thee: "I am not bound by form of man, for I have earned by eternal freedom, and I am "free born" - born of God, the Father, Am I - I am not bound by the atomic form of man, I go and come at will"

I say: "I am Master of the elements, I am the master of My element! I am Spirit! And I take any form which suits My purpose. I am form! I am the one sent of God, the Father, for a purpose, and that is His will - that I be free - even as He is free. I say unto thee: "O, Children of Israel, I come that ye be brought out of bondage, have ye not been bound long enough?" And I say: "Ye have forgot thy royal lineage, ye are of the House of David and ye are therefore the chosen of God, the Father!"

Ye have wandered long and far! And I say unto thee: "O, Royal Sons of the House of David, ARISE! Sluff off thy lethargy, thy slothfulness and cut away thy leg-irons, cast them off! Bare thy hear and cast aside thy black hood - thy robes of black! Check thine impulse to rend asunder thy benefactors which have kept thee for this day of atonement."

Yet O, Mighty Ones of Israel, I say unto thee: "Ye shall come unto Me - and ye shall clean thine own altar! Thy hands and thy heart shall be pure." For I say unto thee: "Ye shall not barter with Me - for the Father hath sent Me - that ye may have a new dispensation, and a new law, and I bring it unto thee!

I say: "Ye have gone the long way to deny Me! Yet ye shall be as ones which have thrown overboard thine own life belt!" I speak unto thee as one of old - yet I speak unto thee of the law which is 'new' yet ever has it been from the beginning.

Now ye shall be unto thyself true, and ye shall heed my words - for I say: "Ye shall be as ones which have thrown overboard thine own life-belt, when ye deny Me, and the word which I bring unto thee!" For I say unto thee: "I am sent of the Father God, the God of Israel!

"O, Sons of Israel, ye have been given a new dispensation, a new law! Ye are no longer under the old law! Ye are now in the new day - the day of salvation, is now come! Make Haste and bless this day, for I say unto thee that I am come as of old, that ye may be brought out of bondage."

"It is nigh upon thee that ye shall be faced with trying times!" Thy labors shall avail thee naught and thy coin shall be as naught, and ye shall weep as with acid which burns thine eyes. I say that ye shall weep. tears of acid which shall sear thine eyes! So be ye not as fools which hath betrayed thyself!

"Arise! And come unto Me! For I say, I now stand ready to bring thee out of bondage!" I am Sananda -

My Strange Act

Beloved: My words shall go into all the nations of the Earth - and they shall fall on fertile soil and take root, and bring forth fruit - I say unto thee, fruit of a NEW variety - fruit which shall nourish the people thereof, and it shall be food for the Spirit - through Spirit and of Spirit.

And I say, that it is near the time when I shall bring forth "My Strange Act" for it is now come when great shall be the works of the Almighty GOD!

I say unto thee - HIS hand is not staid - neither is He bound by man's limitations - man which knows not his power and might - He shall bring forth the babes from the breast to do HIS work, which shall confound the wise, I say <u>they</u> which <u>think</u> themself wise shall be confounded by the wisdom of the babe, which has not the years accredited unto their learning.

I say, they shall be dumbfounded, and confused by their own stupidity! Be ye as ones prepared for the greater part - for it is now come when ye shall go into a place wherein ye shall find one which has his hand in mine and he shall give unto thee a plan wherein there shall be brought forth from the great unknown the things which are necessary unto thy part of the plan.

Now I say unto thee - this one has not as yet spoken unto thee - neither hast thou come together this time - for I say this that the wrong interpretation may not be placed upon these MY WORDS - and for this do I make this clear - for therein is much danger, when they interpret my words to fit into their own preconceived opinions, for therein is folly. Be ye as one enlightened of me, and ye shall know, and ye shall be brought out of darkness.

I say I am not bound by their opinions or preconceived ideas for therein is BONDAGE! Let thy own unknowing trip thee up NOT! For therein is the great test of thy faith- be ye at peace - Patience is no LITTLE part of it - love them which revile thee and give unto them nothing they can use against thee - for they shall come to know the foolishness of their childishness - Let them out-grow it, and they shall come to the age of accountability.

I have said I shall give unto them as they are prepared to receive - I am Sananda

Recorded by Sister Thedra of the Emerald Cross

BY THEIR FRUIT...

Beloved of my being: I say unto the I am thy Lord thy God which hast spoken unto thee, and I say, that I am now prepared to give unto thee the greater part and too, I say, that the time is come when thou shall be blest as I have been blest.

Ye shall now give unto them this My Word, and they shall remember it and keep it immaculate - HOLY they shall not contaminate or defile it for I say unto them woe unto any man which contaminates or adulterates My Word - for I have prepared myself for this part and I am not of a mind to have words put into My Mouth.

So be it that I am not bound, I speak for myself, and too, I say I need no interpreter, for have I not prepared thee to receive of Me and by Me? Yet I say that I am bound by Me Love, to be unto Myself true, true to My Trust.

And I have given unto them My word, that as they are prepared so shall they receive - Now let it be recorded, that I am not deceived, neither do I deceive, nor do I mislead them.

Yet I say unto thee - there are ones among them who have put words into My Mouth - for they have given unto themself credit for being wise: They THINK themself wise and they have not the comprehension of Me.

And I say unto the, My Servants, boast not of their accomplishments, they are not puffed-up. They are as little children, looking unto the Father for sustenance, and I say they are not braggarts.

And while I am about it I shall say that I am not a coward! I say what I will!! And what the Father WILLS, and what the Father would have Me say. I need no mediator! For I am come unto thee for the purpose of enlightening thee - I need none other - for I am capable and I say I am prepared for this part and it is given unto Me to see them strut and boast: and I say, they babble as a foolish children and they know not that which they say.

Be ye as one prepared for the greater part, be ye at peace and poise and I am with ye and ye with Me. I shall not forsake thee.

I am thy Brother and thy Sibor - Sananda.

Recorded by Sister Thedra of the Emerald Cross

The Father's Ultimatum to Men of Earth

My plan I reveal unto My Sons: For they are loyal unto Me, and they have earned the right to call themself "SON" and I say unto them which have turned from Me - they shall not partake of My plan, My wisdom, My house, until they have turned from their own way of bigotry, idolatry, hypocrisy, and the way of the wanton.

I say unto them, ye shall now alert thyself and pick up thy feet, and make haste unto Me, thy Father, for the day draws nigh when the rocks shall tumble and the waters shall flow over thy cities, and thy country as little play-toys.

I say all thy wisdom shall avail thee naught - for I say unto thee which have turned from Me, and spat upon MY WORDS, and MY

PROPHETS which I have brought forth as thy benefactors, ye shall be found wanting, for ye have been as fools - in thy wanton, and in thy idolatry.

Ye have set up images and worshiped them while ye have denied ME, MY POWER and ye have betrayed thyself and thy offspring and ye have sold thy birthright for a puny penny!

Now HEAR ME - Oh, ye foolish ones! And think NOT that MY hand is shortened, nor that I SLEEP! Judge ME NOT BY THY STANDARDS - THY PRECONCEIVED IDEAS OF ME!

For I am not of a mind to play second best - for I AM ALL! I AM that which has brought thee forth and I AM a loving FATHER, yet I AM a wise One: I AM WISDOM and too, I say I have given unto thee free-will, and I shall not trespass upon it, yet I say, I shall cut thee off and cast thee into utter darkness when ye have gone so far as to set thyself up to be the law - FIRST and LAST - for I say, I AM the ALPHA, and the OMEGA!

Yet ye comprehend Me not, and ye have given unto the unknowing ones great and fancy documents about Me, and My laws, ye have confused them by thy dogmas, and thy creeds, ye have wars, and rumors of wars - and ye slay for the gaining of the coin - the wealth of the Earth has been pilfered, and for the ones which sit in high places they make of my servants - slaves!

I say it is finished! I Am thy Father, and I say I Am alert and I Am not of a mind to see My handiwork go for naught - So be ye as ones which have a mind to hear that which I say unto thee! For My day is Come NOW!

HEAR ME! OH, YE CHILDREN OF EARTH! For My hand moveth upon the land, upon the sea, in the firmaments! - and I say I AM not limited for the Earth and the fullness thereof is MINE! Now ye shall be as ones warned of Me and by Me, thy Father, which has given unto thee being - I say I AM ALL POWERFUL, ALL-WISE, and MERCIFUL. My love abideth forever and I say unto thee, return unto Me and receive the fullness thereof. I am Solen Aum Solen.

Recorded by Sister Thedra of the Emerald Cross

Sananda Prays to The Father

Mighty AM I, and My handiwork shall be seen and recognized as <u>mine</u>, throughout all the lands: for I am now come into the Earth in flesh and bone - of flesh and bone am I that these things may be accomplished NOW! In this day when man rushes hither and yon, seeking entertainment and seeking self-aggrandizement, self-sensation - senses of the physical that satisfy -

Yet I ask of thee - WHEREIN ARE THEY SATISFIED? Are they not to be pitied?

I say unto thee be ye as one called out from among them - and be ye as no part of their foolishness: for they are as ones first and last in the dragon's den - they are not aware that I am come - they know not that there is Light for the asking, for the seeking, for the preparation.

I say unto thee that they are not of a mind to hear that which is said unto them from out the realms of Light, for they are as ones blinded by their importance - they ask not for the greater part - they ask not for wisdom.

Yet I say unto thee, great shall be their wailing, and their cries when the great day comes! And I say that they shall seek out the ones which have warned them, which have been the ones to sacrifice for them, and too, I say the ones which have made the sacrifice shall be as ones removed while they shall be as ones found wanting - and they shall not find My Servants wanting - for they shall be as ones prepared for the greater part - for they shall be caught up with Me and they shall be blest as I am blest, as I have been blest of My Father - which has sent Me.

I speak unto thee for their sake, and I say unto them, that they are a sad lot! and they shall be as traitors unto themself, when they deceive themself, and when they do not heed that which has been said unto them.

I am now in physical form, and that form is of Earth, yet it binds Me not - for I am eternally free while I am in the Earth form, I shall walk among thee as man, yet I am no less a Son of God, which hast sent Me, I am free, unbound by flesh or form, for I am not of Earth. I go and come freely, for I am free, I am a free-born man and I have received My inheritance IN-FULL. So be it and Selah.

I come at this time that there may be peace among thee - Oh, ye children of Earth arise, and come home! What shall I do Father! What shall I do, to awaken thy suffering children who have denied thee and turned from thee? Cursed are they, or their own wanton are they cursed! Father! Oh, Father! Give unto them comprehension and I ask it for their sake, AWAKEN THEM!

Be ye not as One cast down, My Son, for I am thy Father, and I am One with them even as I am One with Thee - thou hast come unto them out of thy compassion for the weary and the oppressed, and I say unto Thee, My Son, I shall give unto Thee as Ye have not received, for I say I have yet another part for Thee - Yea, even greater than all which Thou hast received.

Behold ME! My Son, and ye shall be like unto Me upon the Earth, and ye shall be ME, made manifest and ye shall walk the Earth as one unbound - as one come from the Celestial Realms, beyond time and space limitations.

I say unto them which sitteth in high places, I Am the God of Earth and the firmaments thereof - for I have created them. Have I not sent thee, My Son to deliver thee out? Have I not raised up My Holy Ones from among Thee? Have I not given unto thee comfort in thy days of thy youth? Have I not comforted thee in thy affliction? Have I not kept thee for this day?

Yet, oh, wayward Children, I say unto thee - days there are few which ye have - for I have said unto thee that I shall cut thee off and cast thee into utter darkness while it is yet time I say unto thee: My Love is boundless, yet my hand is firm upon thee and ye stand not alone for were it so, I should let thee go - yet MY CHILDREN, ye are not alone! For as one member of My body is afflicted so doth the others suffer - it is better that I cast off the ailing parts, lick my wounds and heal them and grow anew!

I say I have given unto thee being - and I shall give unto thee that which thou hast prepared thyself for to receive - It is the law and I AM thy Father - I AM the Law and I AM the Creator, and I create well - I do not give unto thee of the bitter cup. It is of thy own will - thy own choosing.

And too, I say, I have sent this Mine Son, unto thee for the last time, that ye may be brought out of bondage - that ye may be given thy inheritance in full, that ye may return unto Me with Him and by His grace shall ye come, for I say unto thee, My foolish ones, He is the door through which thou shall enter into My place of abode, for He, I have sent even as I - and I am not He - yet He is ME and we are one - One and the same, - for I have begat HIM, as My first born have I sent Him - that ye may be spared from the great and dreadful pit!

Let not thy opinions belie My words, or lead thee astray. Let not thy leaders beguile thee as they are beguiled by the one cast down. Heed ye MY Words - My Children and ARISE, COME HOME! And I shall receive thee unto Myself and I shall be glad thy sojourn is ended forever for I have given unto thee a new dispensation - and a new law and I have sent unto thee a host of Angelic Ones - from out the realms of Light have they descended to arouse thee - to be with thee in this thy hour of trial, for trial there shall be and ye shall be as ones prepared.

For it is now come when great changes shall come about and every state, every country, every nation, every part of the Earth shall feel the action thereof, for thy "little mind" cannot conceive of such changes, and they shall come in rapid succession and I say rapid! For there is the great flood which ye have recorded and it was so, that they were warned! and it is the law that they be warned ere they are destroyed.

Now remember this - to retain thy physical form is not enough, yet is the better part, for to lose it ere thy mission is finished is pity, for therein is another story - and therein another day. Yet ye shall be wise to alert thyself - ARISE, and recover thy memory and let it be done, finished! For I say unto them they which doth return unto me shall have their memory restored unto them, and they shall never again take embodiment through the womb of woman - and they shall be as ones free from the wheel of rebirth forever, So be it as thou will it.

I AM thy Father Eternal and through My Love, My mercy, and grace I have sent unto thee a host of My Angelic forces that ye may suffer no more. I AM finished this day - SELAH - Peace be with thee - MY peace I bestow upon thee - Be ye blest of Me and of My Sons which I have sent. Be ye blest of this My daughter, which I have sent for I say unto thee hers is no small part - for I have made her the keeper of the keys - So be it and SELAH.

My Father has spoken, and I am satisfied - I bless thee as He would have ME -

I say unto thee My Beloved, I bow unto thee - and I give unto thee of My love - MY strength, that ye may be sustained, and by HIS mercy and grace I am permitted to come unto thee. So be it and SELAH, I AM HIS Son, Sananda -

Recorded by Sister Thedra of the Emerald Cross

* Flood of 'Noah

Memory and The Spoken Word

Father Mother God; I Thedra, bring these supplications of Thy children, to this Thy altar which Thou hast brought forth, in THY

NAME, - I come - that they may be blest of Thee - THY WILL BE DONE ---

By Mine hand shall they be blest, for have I not given unto them life? Wherein have I been found wanting - wherein have I denied them and wherein have I cut them off?

They have wandered from Me, and they are as ones in darkness; for I say they remember Me NOT - yet they ask not to have their memory restored -- I say unto thee: their memory contains all knowledge and wisdom known unto man - and therein are the records of their BEGINNING - and the knowledge of their end - that is their Earthly end - for there is NO END to thy "BEING" which I have given unto thee/ them - and when they are so prepared for this great illumination of memory - the <u>restored wisdom</u> - they shall receive it in full ---

Now while it is yet time - I say unto them they shall be as ones prepared to receive this precious gift, which I have held in trust for them and ye shall be wise indeed to prepare thyself for to receive it ---

Now I shall ask of them - wherein have they hidden all their deeds all their secrets - wherein have they buried the past - wherein have they stored their treasures - wherein have they hidden their sorrows wherein have they placed that which they will to remember - and that which they will to forget? ---

I say unto them: open up thy secret place, and look therein, and behold that which is stored therein, and then I say unto them be ye as one wise to clean it out - and empty it! clean it out! and place therein <u>only</u> that which shall profit thee - each item therein shall be examined and seen for that which it is - and then discarded as an old worn out garment - long since useless, do not drag the debris - the trash - the filth, with thee - for it is as a pack upon thy back, and as legirons about thy feet - let not these things deter thee upon thy path ---

Now it is well, that I speak unto thee of thy words - for when ye use them, do so wisely, and be sure of them, for they go out from thee as <u>living things</u>; and once they leave thy lips they begin to grow as the virus; for they fall on fertile soil - that of <u>mind</u> and when the spurious mind receives these idle words they grow as a cancer - and an ugly thing - to be as a contamination, and a blight upon thy own existence - and therein is the <u>greatest</u> of folly!

I say unto them when thy words are of truth, and when they leave thy lips as such they shall find their place and return unto thee, bearing fruit, which shall nourish and comfort thee it shall be unto thee thy crown - thy shield - thy buckler - thy halo - thy seamless garment, which thou dost construct with thine own hands thy own will. Now I say unto thee be ye aware of the spoken word - and bless thyself thereby -- I am thy Elder Brother – Berean.

I Stood Upon Mt. Golgotha

Beloved: I stood upon Mt. Golgotha, that I might prove unto them a law; which they never had been prepared to accept: while they saw the other side of the aspect, that aspect of Earth - the negative aspect - they did not realize the fullness of that act - that DIVINE DRAMA, which was acted out through the ones which are within the Earth (upon the Earth) this day for the final act.

I say that they which were with me are back this day for the final act - and I say this is the final act of this show - for it is now the eleventh hour of the last day - I say the midnight striketh, and I find them asleep.

Yea, the dawn of the new day cometh and they sleepeth! I find them disorderly - within their torn and worn beds: ragged and begotten of wear - and be ragged with time, and worse for their dreams.

I find them in their nakedness, and dirty with sweat, and worn with care, fraught with pain and passion - and they call unto their physicians, for relief; yet they ask of the Father naught; for they know Him NOT!

Yet I say unto thee my Beloved: I am come that they may know Him, for this do I come unto thee, that ye may be MY VOICE, MY hands, MY feet, and I say too, that MY VOICE shall be heard in ALL lands of the Earth, ALL the waters of the seas, and the firmaments there roundabout: for I come bringing with me a host of mine company, (the heavenly host, if you like) and I shall say unto thee, they are of the "ROYAL ASSEMBLY" for I know them.

I too say that this is the great day, for which ye have waited the day of cleansing, purification, action, finish, the day of completion, rejoicing, returning unto the place of thy abode.

Now beloved: I say unto them, which have betrayed themselves, and which do 'think' themselves wise, that they shall be caught up short; and they shall be found wanting - for too I say that there are ones among thee which would hold thee in bondage by their dogmas - their creeds, opinions, their own wonton (rebelliousness).

Now let me say this, while there is yet time, I am come that this may end! And I say I am well prepared, and I am not of a mind to be tray myself, nor my trust, for my Father has sent me that this foolishness be finished!

Each has volunteered for his part - and passed the great BOARD, (the Board of Directors, if you will) and they have come with the consent of the great fraternal Brotherhood, which ye call the "White Brotherhood" and I say it is well said: for by their Light dost thou see thy way, by the grace of the Father which hast sent me, are they endowed their Sonship, which is their freedom, to choose this part, for this are they permitted this part in the great plan. They come and go freely, let it be understood, when they choose - accept - and do come on such a mission - (assignment, if you will) they never, never turn back, until it is finished!

I say finish it; and that is the better part of wisdom! I say they betray NOT their trust!

Mighty is HIS love, great HIS mercy, and peaceful HIS means: yet, I say unto the wanton ones, they shall receive as they are prepared, for it is the law.

I say as they have sown so shall they reap, they shall receive in like measure - Be ye as ones prepared to receive the better part.

I come that ye be lifted up, and I come that ye be brought out of bondage.

I bless thee with my presence - I leave thee in peace, be ye as my hand unto them, and great shall be thy reward - give this unto them in my name, and sign it as my servant, whom I have chosen; for thy grace, and for thy loyalty.

I am Sananda.

Behold me! Thy Lord, Thy God!

I stand upon my high holy Mt. and I say unto thee; I AM thy Lord, thy God, which hast brought thee forth as an individual beings, endowed of free will, and I have fed thee from mine own hand.

I have held thee within my hand fast! that ye may know that I am thy God - yet thou hast been away from me long.

Now ye shall return unto me and be satisfied, I say ye shall return unto me and be satisfied, for this have I placed mine seal upon thee - I say unto thee I am thy Father, which has sent thee forth as mine child, now I call thee home - and thou hast heard me, and turned thy fact homeward - So be it that I shall receive thee, and I shall be glad, be blest this day of me, and by me, I AM thy Father,

Solen Aum Solen.

Recorded by Sister Thedra

My Children of Earth
Come Home, Come Home!

Beloved Children of Earth: I say unto thee this day; ARISE, COME HOME, COME HOME! For long hast thou wandered in darkness and in bondage.

And I say unto thee my Children; it is thy own will - thy own rebelliousness, thy own wonton, which holds thee bound. Be ye no longer bound by thy dogmas, thy creeds, thy preconceived ideas/ opinions - and turn unto me, wholeheartedly, with thy whole being! with ALL thy will, give unto me recognition, THE SOURCE OF THY BEING, from whence thou hast gone out.

OH, MY CHILDREN: Could ye but cut away thy legirons! thy preconceived ideas of me, created by man's illusions - man's opinions of me thy FATHER, thou wouldst arise and make haste unto me!

I say unto thee: Blest are they which return unto me this day, for great shall be their reward - Now be ye as ONE of them, for thou shall receive of me thy Sonship, thy inheritance in full, and ye shall wander in darkness no more; nor have I willed it so; thou hast gone into darkness of thy own free will, yet I say unto thee ye shall arise and return of thy own free will.

Now I say unto thee this day: I have given unto thee LIFE, and FREEWILL, and I say I shall not trespass upon thy precious gift! Yet when thou dost use it for thy own deliverance, and with ALL thy strength, all thy mind turn unto me with a contrite heart, and the way is open - and I have sent unto thee thy Wayshower - and many have I sent to point the way, and I speak through them unto thee, as of OLD, for I AM thy Father ETERNAL - I weary not of well doing; for I AM a loving Father, and I hold thee fast, yet I wait that ye may return unto me of thy own will.

I say, I have sent MY EMISARRIES, without number that ye may have my words and know my will - yet when thou hast prepared thyself for such as I have kept for thee, I shall give it unto thee AS YE ARE PREPARED, SO SHALL YE RECEIVE - It is the law.

And I say, blest is he which receives of me, and by me, for he shall see me face to face, he shall dwell in my place of abode, for I have kept a place for him.

I say unto thee, MY WAYWARD CHILDREN! thou art a frail lot a sad lot! For thou hast forfeited thy inheritance!

And I say unto thee; ye have but to arise from thy lethargy thy sleep, thy unknowing, and follow him, which I have sent unto thee - NOW HEAR ME, MY CHILDREN! and HEED well these MY WORDS: that I have sent MINE SON unto thee with his host of ten thousand times ten thousand Angels. Now he is come, NOW he walks the Earth, as of OLD; he has filled his covenant with thee, and he has returned; he has been diligent, and he has been unto himself true - unto his trust true - he hast returned and I say unto thee, my UNKNOWING CHILDREN: I speak unto thee out of compassion for thee - for do I not know thy frailties - thy weakness? Yet when thou dost seek the Light, the source of thy Being, it shall not be denied thee; for I shall send unto thee a host of mine Angelic forces to contribute unto thy knowing -

Now My Children: I say unto thee; ye walk in bondage, in darkness each preconceived idea, each opinion ye have of me and about me, thy Father, is another link in thy legirons, which doth bind thy feet.

Now I say unto thee: I AM limitless

I AM ALL powerful

I AM Omnipresent

I AM the ALL

I AM SPIRIT

I AM matter

I give

I take

I rest not

I AM rest

I go not, yet

I AM there

I AM here

I go not into the darkness, yet out of the darkness cometh LIGHT - I AM NOT thee; thou art not me I have brought thee hence, from my own breath, breathed upon that form which I imaged, which I willed.

Now let this be recorded within these scripts NOW, that I have willed thy form, which I didst fashion, yet that form, the garment of flesh is but that which thou weareth for a time - then it shall be discarded for yet another more glorious and perfect!

Ye shall wear the ROYAL raiment not made of matter, ore atomic substance of Earth, for I say; ye, and ye alone, shall transmute ALL thy misused energy and stand forever free from the gravitation of the Earth and the attraction of the Moon. Ye shall place thy hand in mine and I shall bless thee as I have blest him, which I have sent unto thee - for have I not given unto him power over the elements, over the Earth, and the fullness thereof? I say ALL I have is his, is thine, yet ye shall prepare thyself for to receive the fullness of MY estate.

I AM thy Father, Solen Aum Solen, Bless thyself as ye would have me bless thee.

Recorded through HIS GRACE, by Sister Thedra

Wisdom

Behold ME! This day I stand before thee - see me - walk with me - Say unto them - I AM come - I AM here - I AM he which hast returned, I am he that hast prepared a place for them - wherein it is written: "I go to prepare a place for thee?" To whom didst I say these words? To thee, mine Children, to thee! Where didst thou tarry? Wherein hast thou been? Wherein hast YE BEEN?

Yet, yet many be ones which did NOT!

Have ye remembered thy waiting? Have ye had the fortune of remembering me and have ye been so fortuned as to have thy memory restored thee? Have ye given thought unto these things?

Let me ask of thee ONE THING, have ye been true unto thyself? Have ye been unto thy trust true? Blessed are they which have!

I say blessed are they which have; for unto them the VICTORY! Blessed shall they be, I say unto thee be ye as one of these, for it is the Father's WILL that ye return unto HIM this day - I say THIS DAY for there are NO tomorrows!

This day is thine! Use it to do thy good work; and to justify thyself; even as ye shall be justified by thine good works, for by thy works shall ye be judged, and by thy works shall ye be weighed in the balance.

Should ye be found wanting, some other, shall pick up thy part and receive the reward thereof for I say unto thee great is the blessing of a part well chosen and carried out unto its completion!

For the day is now come when there is much to do - and great the labor - as well as the reward - there are none so weak, none so blind, so low, which has not something to contribute unto the Fathers plan - I say they all have a part - while there are none great, none small, there are various parts within the great plan, and some have fulfilled that part; yet they have chosen yet another that ye may walk the Royal Road by their GRACE: their help which is available unto thee for the asking, and sufficient preparation.*

Now be ye as one prepared to receive of them, and by them; for ye shall be blest as they are blest - and by their GRACE, shall ye receive thy own grace - I say unto thee these art thy Benefactors which have gone before thee.

Now when they know the wisdom of such learning, and the great JOY of such accomplishments, they do that which other hast done for them; they hold out a hand unto thee that ye may walk by their light - so be it the law - and I say unto thee it is the law of LOVE and PEACE, HARMONY, therein is no vicarious atonement; each is responsible for himself, his own salvation - yet, I say: as he prepares himself so shall he receive. These which hast gone the ROYAL ROAD, only assist in lifting him up, and I say they ONLY assist, in raising him up.

And I say unto them; blest are they which have gone the ROYAL ROAD; and which do assist thee: I AM one which knows, be ye blest of me and by me, I am thy Sibor and thy Brother Bernard.

Recorded by Sister Thedra

*The work of the White Brotherhood after they have won their freedom, choose to assist us.

When This is Done

Beloved: Upon My high holy Mt. I stand: I behold thee in thy effort to reach them - I see them sleeping midstream - I see them within their slumbers, dreaming dreams which torment them; I say unto them "AWAKEN!" they hear me not! I call unto them, they close me out; they are calloused, they have hardened their hearts, they have turned from me, they have not ears to hear, nor eyes to see, they are blind unto me, and deaf unto my call.

Now I say unto them, they shall awaken, for I shall awaken them! For I shall give unto them a portion which they shall understand: and it shall shake them into consciousness awakening - they shall bestir themself; and arise, and come forth from their tomb!

And they shall walk upright, with surety, and with dignity, they shall be as ones awakened! Now they are as ones in a state of lethargy; a state of confusion: unknowing - they sleep the sleep of the wonton; they rebel at the thought of being awakened!

They are not satisfied - yet they know not where to find satisfaction: they are wandering in darkness, and they are as ones lost - bound by their own rebelliousness (wonton).

I say sad is their plight! Yet I have not willed this - neither has MY Father, He has sent HIS Emissaries, His Sons, that He may awaken them; and now I say ACTION shall be taken; taken for their sake- and they shall have that which is necessary to awaken them; for this is the day of action! While it is yet time, I say unto thee My Beloved ye shall see this come about - for it is now time that they awaken; And they shall be as ones rudely awakened!

For they are so deep in sleep that nothing short of a rude awakening will stir them - I say they shall be as ones thrown out of their bed - they shall find themself wet in their bed - they shall find themselves in the place wherein they are as ones confused and dumbfounded; and they shall find their homes overturned, and in shambles - they shall be as one maimed, and tormented with pain and with no physician!

They shall have no communication with each other - and they shall call out and not be heard! Yet I say unto them; they have time to prepare themself for that which shall come upon them. I have warned them; many times; yet I say they have not given unto ME credit for that which I AM, or, that which I say unto them! Now ye shall give unto them these MY WORDS, and too, I say that they shall say: "IT IS SO!"

I say unto them: YE FOOLS: now is the day of preparation, and all which are prepared shall be given unto according to their preparation for it is the law: "AS YE ARE PREPARED, SO SHALL YE RECEIVE." Now should ye ARISE, and return unto me ye shall be delivered out - ye shall know no want, no mystery - yet, should thou goest headlong into this, ye shall be as which hast thrown overboard thy own lifebelt. Yet ye shall be as one which has betrayed thy ownself; for I say unto thee; MY FIRST COMMANDMENT UNTO THEE is; "BE YE TRUE UNTO THYSELF: WALK IN THE WAY I LEAD THEE"

When this is done, thou shalt walk in the way I lead thee - and too I say; I AM sent of the Father that ye may be led out of bondage ; that ye may return unto thy abiding place, to go into darkness no more. I say, that ye shall return in due time, yet Blessed is he which doth return unto HIM this day; for it is the day for which thou hast waited, and now I find thee wanting, and within thy beds sleeping!

I say unto thee; thy foolishness shall cease, and ye shall shake off thy lethargy and come with me - yet ye shall will it so - for I shall not trespass upon thy own free will - and it is not lawful, that one trespass upon another, not even the father of ALL will do this, and HE is the LAW, LOVE is HE, and HE is merciful beyond comprehension: and He is WISDOM; and JUDGEMENT, belongs unto HIM: NONE OTHER!

Be ye as one prepared to receive me, and of me, and I shall lead thee into the place wherein ye shall find surcease from pain and suffering of any kind - wherein there is no darkness, no want. I say ye shall know - and know that ye know, and great shall be thy joy - praise ye the name of the Father/Mother GOD, Solen Aum Solen, the day is come - I walk among thee in flesh and bone; and I am here that ye may go where I go, that ye may be as I AM, that ye may return unto HIM the FATHER, with me, so be it a great day of rejoicing, I AM HIS SON, sent to bring thee, I AM Sananda, the Nazerine.

Alpha and Omega

Beloved of my being: I speak unto thee simply, yet firmly; for I am not of the Earth, for I AM ALL that is; which is everlastsing; from everlasting, unto everlasting, I AM the ALPHA and the OMEGA, - I AM thy Father Eternal, which hast given unto thee BEING.

Now I say unto thee great and glorious is my handwork, for I have set the planets upon their course, I have given unto thee SUN by day - the Moon by night; and I have given unto thee starts, that ye may be kept thereby –

I have given unto thee a part which shall be finished - I have given unto thee a commandment: the first: "REMEMBER ME AND RETURN UNTO ME." and ye shall be as one blest - for I say that it is now come when great and mighty things shall be revealed unto thee; and ye shall be as one prepared, for it is now come when mine Son shall come unto thee and he shall bless thee as none other: for I say that he has the power and the authority to bless thee as I have blest him now I say unto thee be ye as one prepared to receive him and of him. Let thy peace be my peace –

Let thy mind be my mind - let thy will be my will - let thy words be my words - let thy work be my work - let thy hands be my hands - let thy feet be my feet - let thy days be my days: and I say unto thee thy reward shall be great indeed! I have spoken and thou hast heard me; ye shall be as one brought out of bondage, for this have I spoken unto thee, I AM thy Father ETERNAL, Solen Aum Solen,

Received by Sister Thedra

Ye Shall Father Thy Own Child

Beloved: I say unto thee, I am thy Lord thy God, and I now speak unto thee this day that they may awaken, and that they may arise, and be alert unto that which goes on about them; for this is the time which is come now - which they have waited for: and now they are within the dens of iniquity; and within the places of entertainment, wherein they find naught but wonton, and willfulness, wherein they do serve the dragon with all their might!

I say, that I shall cut them off! I shall lay waste their citadels; I shall place my seal upon this; for I am of a mind to clean them out! I say I am NOT of a mind to give unto them energy, that they may use for the destruction of mine work; of mine handiwork. I shall show MY hand! for I am not asleep! I say that they set into motion that which shall rebound upon them; for they have given little thought unto the law, which is set before them.

Now I say unto them; YE shall be as the ones which have unleashed the power which thou hast misused; now it shall return unto thee a-thousand fold, bearing upon it the likeness of thy own handiwork, and bearing the fruit thereof.

Now let it be UNDERSTOOD, that "YE FATHER THY OWN CHILD" and none shall deny him; for ye alone have begotten him: and when he is begotten in whoredom, thou alone shall pay for thy own folly: and I say unto thee, ye have begotten the one which ye call 'Satan' ye have begotten him!

For I say unto thee, he has no power over thee against thy own will, he is helpless to hold thee against thy own will - yet I say unto thee ye shall transmute all thy misused energy which thou hast set into motion! And therein is thy salvation - for none other can do it for thee; be ye not so foolish as to think so; for it is not the law.

I say: ye shall transmute ALL thy misused energy; and ye shall atone for every part of thy way: every place wherein thou hast sown seeds of discord, ye shall gather together that energy and transmute it!

Now I say unto thee; ye shall be led into the places wherein ye have sown such seeds and ye shall be shown that which thou hast forgotten and ye shall remember these things, and ye shall be as ones prepared for these things, for I say unto thee, that it is now time that ye acquaint thyself with the law on such things.

For ye have been kept in bondage, and ye know not these things: for thy churches, tabernacles, and synagogues tell ye not of these things; for they would that ye walk in darkness!

NOW I say unto thee ye shall stand face to face with thyself; and ye shall know that which ye have done - and ye shall know that which prompted the doing! And ye shall forgive thyself, and make haste to remedy thy wrongs; and by so doing, love thyself free: ye shall bless them, as ye have been blest, ye shall rectify ALL thy wrongs! And in case they are no longer within thy sight, within thy reach - thy hearing, ye shall forgive them all their trespasses, and ask forgiveness of them, as though they stood before thee! And in SPIRIT it shall be so! For I say: "SO ABOVE, SO BELOW" Yet in Spirit there is no time - no distance - no separation, and it is so. So be it and Selah.

Now ye shall be as one prepared for thy own forgiveness - for I say unto thee: EXPECT NOT FORGIVENESS, SO LONG AS THOU

HOLDEST ONE JOT OR TITTLE AGAINST ANOTHER!! For therein is thy own forgiveness: Ask NOT forgiveness, before thou hast forgiven them which hast 'sinned' against thee - for I say unto thee therein is thy own release from bondage, so be it and SELAH.

I am ready to speak unto thee of LOVE, yet another day. I am with thee - lovest thou ME? I am Sananda.

Recorded by Sister Thedra

Priest Craft

By My hand shall ye be led this day, and by My hand shall ye receive this part which I am about to give unto thee; now ye shall put thy whole heart and mind into this part: for I say unto thee it is for them which have a mind to learn, and to be brought out of bondage.

I say unto them: I am now come to reveal unto them the Lord thy God which hast hidden his face from them - and I come that they may be unbound - that they may have truth abundantly, and that they may be free forever more - I say forever free!

I come to unleash them from their dogmas, creeds, from their superstitions, opinions, preconceived ideas: yet I say unto thee My Beloved they have clung unto their leg-irons for so long they feel part of them; and they know not that they are bound; so be it that they first come to know that they are bound by their own leg irons - their preconceived ideas of truth; and of me, and that which I bring unto them.

My WORD unto them is without pretense of workmanship - without their 'embellishment' without "Priest Craft' I say unto them: I AM of My Father sent - I bow unto none - except mine servant which I loveth, I bless her as none other!

I say unto thee mine beloved, ye have done this which none other has: (let this be recorded)

I come that they be forever free - and ye shall play a part which shall be given unto thee for this day - this is MY DAY - it shall be thy day; let us call it "OUR DAY" - and ye shall see it come into its fullness, for it is now come when we shall stand side by side and see them brought out; for it is given unto me to foresee this: I know them - and I know wherein to find them: yet I say I shall bring them out their hiding places, and I shall deliver them from the dragons den - and I shall give unto the foolish the cup of living water - I shall lift them up - I shall bring forth the lowly and exalt them - I shall find them in the prisons and free them.

I shall walk among them, and touch them and they shall be quickened - I shall speak the Word and the dead shall leap up, and I shall go forth as one unknown - uncrowned - unrecognized and I shall cause them to awaken - I shall be as one which has the power to turn the water into wine: and the wine shall sober them; and they shall walk upright, and they shall go into their drunken stupor no more. I come that they may be sobered - that they may come alive.

Now let this be recorded for them this day: upon this I set mine seal: I put my words into thy mouth - and I say unto thee My Beloved I AM NOT so foolish as to give unto them MY PEARLS, without price; for

I say they shall prepare themself for to receive me, and of me and they which think otherwise are the foolish ones.

Now I say unto them: I have appointed this mine servant to give unto thee My NEW name Sananda, through her My Father hast revealed HIS Name Solen Aum Solen: and I say that in these words are powers which ye know not of: I say be ye not so foolish as to take them in vain: for it shall be as nothing which thou hast known!

I say the power which these names carry shall rebound upon them which doth misuse them: for it is given unto thee, this commandment "KEEP THEM HOLY, AND IMMACULATE: IMMACULATE IN ITS HOLINESS AND PURITY: ADD NOTHING: TAKE NOTHING AWAY" Be ye forewarned, for I am true unto my trust; and I say I have warned thee, as a mother would warn a child of the element of fire: I say these words are "FIRE" these words are LIFE, and life is fire: set no ill into motion by the misuse thereof; I say I AM thy Brother which hast gone before thee to prepare the way - I am Sananda.

Recorded by Sister Thedra

Knowest Thou Me?

Solen Aum Solen

Be ye my mouth, my voice unto them; say into them, I AM in the place wherein there is no darkness: wherein I shall bring them as they are prepared to receive; and none other shall enter into my place of abode, for there is not one which shall enter unprepared.

Now say unto them: be ye not deceived! For I Am thy Father Eternal and I have given unto thee being - and ye have given unto thyself credit for being wise.

I ask of thee: Knowest thou Me? And I ask of thee; whence comest thou - whither goest thou?

Now when ye knowest the answers unto these things, then, and only then shalt thou be wise!

I say unto thee, which thinkest thyself wise; when thou hast controlled the elements, raised the dead, healed the sick by the spoken word, and given credit where credit is due - then thou shalt be wise.

And I say unto thee; ye first become as a little child; and ye shall be as one prepared for the next part - I say come as a little child, <u>filled</u> with wonderment, and compassion; and ye shall walk circumspect in all thy ways; all thy doing and all thy days shall be given unto graciousness, ye shall be favored by me, for I say thou shall bless thyself, as ye would be blest.

I have endowed unto thee the fullness of my estate and ye have but to accept it.

Now I say unto thee; the fullness of my love abideth with thee; yet thou hast turned a deaf ear unto me; and I have given unto thee commandments which would free thee from all thy bondage forever, yet ye heed them not!

I say, when thou so loveth each other that ye take upon thyself his suffering, his heartache, his bereavement, his sins for his sake thou art prepared for the next step - yet this is not the law; this is

COMPASSION: this is LOVE: this is which comes from suffering: for suffering brings understanding, and compassion one for the other.

I say ye shall torment thyself until this lesson is learned; and it is said, "A LESSON LEARNED IS A LESSON EARNED" So be it and SELAH.

I speak unto thee of TRUTH - of WISDOM - and thou art as yet not prepared to receive the fullness of my love for I say that it is more glorious to give than to receive - and to give thy life that others may live, is better than to deprive another his right of expression; for this is thy own downfall!

I say not one, has the right to take into his hands the life of another living being, or creature: I say, that it is not lawful; for that which he cannot give, he shall not take: neither shall he accept from another that which he <u>would not</u> give.

I say he has not the right to take the life of any living creature be he MAN, or MOUSE.

I say he has done this to his own undoing; Be ye as one warned; and as one alert, for I say, that the time is now come when great Light shall flood the Earth, and all thy misused energy shall be - transmuted; and ye shall make haste this day, for I say that the ones which cannot abide the Light which shall flood the Earth shall be removed by natural law, and they shall endure great suffering and sorrow.

Now HEAR ME, ALL YE CHILDREN OF EARTH!

I AM thy Father Eternal I AM; and I would that ye all return unto me this day and be forever free: and yet, I say that I shall move out the

Earth from her present port into yet another, and she shall go through the purifying fires, she shall be purged from all darkness; all 'sin'; "sin" being darkness: I say she shall be cleansed and purified; and all which is unpure and unholy shall be removed into yet other realms, wherein ye shall be put (ye which hast not purified thyself) and therein ye shall wait another day ere thou hast prepared thyself.

Ye shall return unto Me in due time, and I say make haste, and be ye as one prepared to receive of me thy inheritance in full-I have sent thee My Sons, MY Emissaries, that thou mayest know the law - and that thou mayest return unto me - such is my love for thee,

I AM Thy Father Solen Aum Solen, I am thy Father Eternal.

Recorded by Sister Thedra

Holy Sacrament

Behold ME this day: Look upon MY handiwork and be mindful of ME: give not the forces of darkness credit for mine work, for I say unto thee, I AM thy Lord thy God, from mine own hand hast I brought these things; the Heavens and Earth; yea, the fullness thereof.

I have given thee dominion over that which I didst create perfectly; yet, Oh, Man, what hast thou done with mine handiwork??

I say unto thee, thou hast distorted it in its third magnitude, ye hast been as the wonton children; ye hast gone into the temples which I didst set up, and ye didst place upon the altars thereof graven images, and ye didst place them there in my name; ye didst bow down before them: ye didst eat of bread and wine in my name. I say unto thee, ye are as the foolish! Thou hast as yet, not drunken of the water of Life; nor eaten of the Bread of Life!

OH, ye wanton ones; I say ye hast not partaken of the "HOLY SACRAMENT! for ye know not its meaning!

Thou hast not as yet, comprehended the fullness of mine words; thou hast as yet, not comprehended the WISDOM contained within them: thou as yet, do not see the fullness of mine handiwork!

Oh, ye wanton children; I give unto thee one law - one commandment "RETURN UNTO ME THIS DAY! Put aside thy pettiness; thy little ways; thy own preconceived ideas of thy God; KNOW ME: Oh, MY CHILDREN of Earth. Return unto ME I ASK!"

Grovel within the mire no longer: I shall give unto thee LIFE ABUNDANTLY; more precious than all thy treasure houses of Earth! I say all I have is thine; ARISE! Make haste this day - be ye as one willing to receive of ME mine estate.

I say all I have is thine; ARISE! Make haste this day - be ye as one willing to receive of ME mine estate.

I say ALL I HAVE IS THINE: MAKE HASTE, AND BE AS ONE RETURNED UNTO ME,

I say I AM thy Father Eternal; Eternally I AM: I say unto thee none other shall usurp mine power; nor pilfer mine storehouse!

I say IAM thy Father the giver and the taker - the parent Eternal: I send forth - I bring hence - I go not - neither do I come - yet I will that ye do come hence, and I shall be unto thee all which ye shall have need of.

I say come unto Me and receive of ME thy sonship, thy inheritance in full. I AM Solen Aum Solen,

Recorded by Sister Thedra

They Need Not Suffer

Beloved of My Being: I say unto thee this day, I AM thy Lord thy God, be ye blest of Me and by Me; and be ye my mouth; my voice unto them: and say unto them in my name, and for their sake; that when it is come that great suffering comes upon them that they shall remember that which I have said; and then they shall cry out unto me, and then they shall turn unto me, because of their suffering.

I say unto thee; because of their suffering shall they turn unto me - yet I say they need not suffer: for all which turn unto me this day and do seek me out shall be delivered out before the great day of sorrow and suffering.

I say they need not suffer; for I have not willed it so: so be it that they have been unto themself traitors (them which doth become a part of the coming great catastrophe) Now there are none so foolish as the ones which doth betray themself.

I say that they; and they alone, are responsible for their folly; and they shall pay the price of the foolish; now I say unto thee the foolish are the ones which think themself wise; yet ones of little knowledge:

are the ones which shall be given comprehension, for <u>they</u> know that they know not! While the foolish <u>think</u> they know!

I say that the foolish shall be as the ones which betray themself; they shall call My Prophets fools - yet I shall exalt them over the ones which have given unto themself credit for being 'wise', I shall give unto them WISDOM, which the foolish ones know NOT of! I shall reveal unto them My law - My secrets, which they know not: and I shall make of them "KEEPER OF THE KEYS" I shall lift them up; and I shall place within their hand the scepter, and the orb and therein is power and wisdom.

I say I shall exalt the lowly, and the humble and the just: while I shall cast out the proud and the haughty, and the unjust; I shall bring them low!

I have said: I shall lay low their citadels; and I shall lay waste their land: and I shall confound them, and their days shall be filled with torment, for I shall unleash that which they have held bound. I shall put within their own hand that which they have created.

I say they shall father their own child, be he what he may: I say for weal or woe, they see him for that which he is! Now let it be said that none escapes the law: and they shall be no exception unto the law, for the law plays no favorites!

I say I will they all return unto me this day while it is yet time, WHILE IT IS YET TIME! Yet I find them in the places wherein they lie dying and wherein they stink, and yet they are not of a mind to turn unto me - Yet I find they are not prepared for the fullness of mine inheritance

There are ones which have come into the Earth as mine Emissaries to lessen their sorrow, their suffering: and yet they do not comprehend the way of them which I send; which are come for their good, their deliverance - I say they have endured great hazards, great suffering for their sake - and yet they persecute them unto this day.

Now I say again: THIS SHALL END! For I have sent mine Sons this day that they may bring forth a plan unto them, and they shall accept it or they shall be removed from the face of the Earth; If I say I am not of a mind to see mine handiwork go for naught; I am not at peace with them; they are offensive unto me; they are a blight upon my handiwork - and they doth try me: I say I am finished with them; I shall cut them off - it is better than to have them all perish!

I say I am now finished with them! I have spoken and I am NOT finished; for I shall speak again, and again.

I AM thy Lord, thy God, I AM the law - I AM He which hast created the Earth and the fullness thereof, I AM Solen Aum Solen.

Recorded by Sister Thedra

Maroni Speaks: In the First Magnitude

Behold my face, and know that I AM thy lord thy God; - Behold me - for I AM with thee this day, and I come as one made manifest upon the Earth - I have made manifest myself upon the Earth in physical form - I say I AM in physical form; as male, and I shall be as male, for I shall walk among them as such: I shall grow unto manhood and I shall be as man: I shall be as none other; for I AM not as any other, for I AM the Father God, in the first magnitude.

I say I AM not of the Earth, yet I have taken 'Earth form' form indigenous of 'Earth child' yet I say that form binds me not! Neither shall I be bound by the laws of Earth, for I shall be bound by NOTHING! I say: I AM in the Earth, but not of it; and I shall go out from the Earth at will, yet I shall be given a part which I shall finish ere I leave it, the Earth; for this have I come.

Now ye shall be as ones prepared to receive me, for I shall come unto thee and counsel thee while I AM yet an infant, and as I mature into manhood I shall go out unto them - and I shall counsel them as they are prepared to receive. Now I say; that there is an ordinance, which says, that in the days when the CHURCH has polluted itself with GAIN from the flesh of the lesser brother it shall be demolished!

I say there IS such an ordinance - and it stands!

I say they have BARTERED in the LIFE which they cannot give! And they have plundered MY WARE! They have pilfered MY WORKS; They make a MOCKERY OF MY WORDS: They make of themself traitors, and liars!

I say I AM come to set straight the records, and to clean their altars! I AM not of a mind to betray myself, or, my trust - Let them have these MY WORDS: and I say unto thee I AM responsible for them (these words) and ye shall be responsible for placing them in their hands,

I AM Maroni.

Recorded by Sister Thedra, through HIS grace

He is Come! The King of Kings

Ye shall go into the place wherein there is little light and say unto them: "He is come, He is come!" I say unto thee this day, ye shall go unto them and declare unto them: "He is come" for this do I speak unto thee; declare unto them He is come, in flesh and bone - flesh of flesh and bone of bone!" And I say unto thee My Beloved; He has been sent even as I was; and am sent of the Father so be it and SELAH.

I say I come that they be delivered out of bondage - So He too has come as one of the 'Host' yet He is the KING! He has come with a host of the great ones from the realms of Light - now I say unto thee: MIGHT is He, and Great, is HIS name: and be ye as one which has revealed it unto them My Beloved; I say unto thee great is this one; for he has gone into the world for their sake - that they may be delivered from bondage.

Woe unto anyone where so ever, which doth take HIS name in vain; for l say there is power in the word SOLEN AUM SOLEN; my WORD I give unto thee that they may have Light; that they may receive it; and I say ye shall be as my hand unto them; my voice unto them - and they shall hear me - for I shall raise MY voice unto the hills - upon the land upon the seas, yea, unto the heavens shall I declare HIS coming - yea that He is HERE!

I say, I have come to make way for HIM; and I Am He, which has prepared the way for HIM - now I prepare the way for them, that they too, may be caught up with HIM - for His reign shall be short, that they too, may be caught up with HIM - for His reign shall be short; it shall not be as the ETERNAL DAY - it shall end and it shall be ample time for them to find HIM and give unto HIM credit for that which He is, and He shall be unto them great Light and strength; for He shall give unto them as they are prepared to receive.

I say it is the day for which they have waited - now ye shall place this within the record and make it available unto them: I say they shall not deny these My Words: for I shall cause them to see the folly of their way, which they have chosen.

And they shall release MY PEOPLE: for I say they shall not be held in bondage longer; when they so will their freedom, I am come to set straight MY WORK - MY PART - My part is to separate the wheat from the chaff and I shall burn the chaff - and it shall be no more; for I come to clean away - to make ready the way for HIM which is come through the womb of woman; through the form of Earth, through the portal of flesh and bone.

I say He hast descended from His place of abode into mortal realm of flesh, that this may be done. I say He began this work Long ago; and it is now come when it shall be completed; for He has given unto the SOURCE all His BEING! all He is; is of the Father - the Father made manifest; yet He is not ALL - He has come as man of flesh and flesh containeth not ALL for He is SPIRIT! And Spirit is NOT FLESH! Yet flesh is not Spirit - Yet Spirit animates flesh.

I say it is well that ye know these things; be ye blest by the knowing. I Am He, which has prepared the way; follow ye me, and I shall lead thee, I AM Sananda, Son of God.

I AM, Thedra, the recorder, by HIS Grace.

They Shall Remember Me

Beloved of My Being: This day shall be set aside as our day, in which we shall give unto them this part, and it shall be as none other, for it is the part for which thou hast waited - and I say unto thee, the time of waiting is ended, for there is no time to wait.

I have said great Light shall flood the Earth, and it is so; so let it be and such knowledge shall become common knowledge; and all which doth oppose it and which doth accuse thee (and all others, which are sent of the Father) of heresy shall go forth into realms which they know not of: for they shall be removed - for no longer shall they be an obstacle in the way of the ones which shall follow the ones which hath come into their midst.

I say they shall be removed - for nothing shall interrupt the plan of the Hierarchy, for it is brought forth with might, it is power, as they know not! and I say all their handiwork shall avail them naught - I say their handiwork shall avail them naught, for it shall crumble before their eyes - I say it SHALL CRUMBLE BEFORE THEIR EYES! It shall be as a house built on quicksand; for they have not given credit unto the great and divine plan - they have not reckoned with the Host - they have thought themself wise!

I say unto them; they shall remember ME - and they shall give unto the SOURCE of their BEING credit for their being - and they shall be as ones prepared to participate in the plan and they shall be as ones prepared to receive their inheritance in full, they shall lift up their eyes unto the hills from whence cometh their strength - they shall bow down and give thanks unto HIM which hast given unto them their BEING - and they shall be as ones mindful of them which are sent, that they may have Light - they shall be given the fullness of their inheritance when they are so prepared - and they shall be brought out of bondage, and they shall know no suffering - no sorrow.

Let it be said, that they shall prepare themself- and so be it this day it is the day of preparation: and when it is come, that they stand face to face with themself they shall know what they have done with the energy which hast been allotted unto them, and they shall be faced with their own foolishness - or, as the ones which shall stand fact to face with GOD the Father.-

I say great shall be the joy of them which doth know HIM, and great sorrow of the traitors - I AM come that they know no sorrow - I AM come to deliver out them which have ears to hear, and eyes to see - so shall they be as ones prepared to receive their inheritance.

I AM HE, which is sent that they may know that which hast been kept from them - I say they which doth SIT in HIGH PLACES and call themself 'WISE" know not that which shall be revealed unto the lowly and the just - they shall be blest of. ME as none of them.

I say: I shall lead them into places wherein fools cannot go! I say: I SHALL LEAD THEM INTO PLACES WHEREIN FOOLS CANNOT GO - FOR THEREIN SHALL BE NO FOOLS - NO TRAITORS - none unprepared so be it I have spoken and I shall speak again and again!

I am thy Sibor and thy Brother - Sanat Kumara

Recorded as received, by Thedra, through HIS grace

The Laws

Beloved: This is the time for which thou hast waited, now thy waiting has ended; and we shall give unto them this part, and it shall contain the laws; and they shall live by them as they are given: and not one place shall they be perverted to suit themself, for therein is the greatest of folly.

Now I say unto thee; ye shall give unto them these scripts and laws contained herein as they are given unto thee: I shall not hold thee responsible for that which they do with them; yet I say they shall be responsible for what they do with them - and when they are of a mind to spit upon them they shall be as traitors unto themself and should they will to accept them, and to follow the way which I set before them, the laws of the first magnitude - unadulterated by man - then they shall be as ones prepared to receive ME, and of ME.

And ye, My Beloved; shall be my hands made manifest unto them: say unto them, as I would say, that the KING of KINGS has come - is NOW HERE; in flesh of my flesh, bone of my bone - and He shall go out on the appointed hour - and He shall walk among them; for He is not of the Earth, and He is not of the Nether world - yet He has taken a body of flesh and bone that they may comprehend as they DO comprehend flesh! Yet they shall come to comprehend Spirit, when they are prepared for this do I speak unto them - I say I AM come that they may comprehend SPIRIT - and Spirit is not contained within flesh and bone.

I say SPIRIT animates the pore, or, flesh and bone - I say SPIRIT IS: Flesh is the illusion: put not thy faith in flesh, for it perisheth, and passeth away - I say SPIRIT is everlasting, and passeth not! Yet I say,

Spirit is that which taketh upon itself garments of flesh; and it goes in and out of each garment as time proposeth: and I say the time has come when Spirit shall no more take upon itself MORTAL body upon the Earth - for the Earth shall be cleansed of mortality - it shall put on IMMORTALITY, and it shall be forever free of mortal substance of flesh and its corruption: I say no longer shall the Earth give footing to the mortal; for mortal has been unto her as barnacles; and now she shall be put into a new port and purified and cleansed of all her 'barnacles' and purified and freed from ALL her misery and want, she the Earth cries out in agony! She is in travail with a son which shall be born in a new part of the firmaments - and she shall be as a VIRGIN and she shall bring forth a child which shall glorify her, and that child shall not defile her; and she shall not disown him: and his name shall be called "RIGHTEOUSNESS" - and there shall be great Light within her, and she shall give unto the Sons of GOD footing: and she shall be as a garden which shall be unto them great joy, and they shall have it for their abiding place.

Is it not said that the Sons of God shall inherit the Earth? Is it not so? Yet I say unto thee, ye hypocrites: deceive not thyself: for I say unto thee: there are none so foolish as the ones which betray themself! I say ye shall be brought to account for thy own foolishness; and too I say, ye shall bless thyself as ye Would have the Father bless thee - ye shall not spit on these MY WORDS, for I say unto thee; I am THY Lord, thy God, and I am not to be given the bitter cup! Be ye circumspect in all thy ways, and I shall be mindful of thee - So be it the law - My love abideth forever - and wherein I AM there is no darkness and I AM not deceived by thy puny words, I see thy heart, and I know what prompts them. I AM thy Older Brother, the Nazerine, The Wayshower! Sananda.

How Hast Thou Fallen So Low

Beloved: This day have I spoken unto thee; and I AM now come as one prepared to give unto thee yet another part for them; and as I have said before, there shall be great Light flood the Earth and all who cannot abide it shall be removed by natural law and they shall be put into their own environment wherein they shall wait another day when they are so prepared to receive it; I say their waiting shall be long, and hard!

For they have betrayed themself: they have misused the energy which has been allotted unto them; now that energy shall be transmuted to the last jot and tittle, and none escapes the law. Now let this be recorded there is none which shall escape the law of JUSTICE; for justice shall rule supreme! Justice is the law; and LOVE covers ALL law - inclusive of ALL law is LOVE: for love is that which has brought thee forth; and in love hast thou been given BEING: yet I say: Ye have perverted the law: thou hast given unto thy brothers the bitter cup - thou hast given him GALL for his cup: thou hast given unto him 'VINEGAR' for water to quench his thirst!

YE FOOLS: Hast thou not suffered sufficiently? Knowest thou not the law? I say ye have been unto thyself traitors! And as ye have sown so shall ye reap and as thou hast prepared thyself so shall thou become! Thou hast become a 'RACE' of vipers, and robbers: thou hast begotten the "Whore" thou hast fashioned her; and thou hast called her FAIR! And thou hast bowed down and worshiped at her feet: I say YE FOOLISH ONES, HOW HAST THOU FALLEN SO LOW? I say thou hast turned from thy GOD; and thou hast gone into the dragons den; FOR WHAT? WHAT HAST IT PROFITED THEE? What hast thou found therein? Naught, except misery and want! Ye shall now be reminded of thy foolishness; for I AM come that ye may awaken!

Throw away thy black capes; thy black hoods; bare thy face, that ye may look upon the SON OF GOD! For I say HE walks amongst thee: He has come into thy midst, that ye may find peace. And I say ye shall turn unto thy Source of BEING with a contrite heart, and ask forgiveness for all thy transgressions; and I say unto thee: ye need no flowery words, for thy Father knowest thy heart; thy every thought - even before thou hast uttered thy words: I say, lay aside all thy hypocrisy and idle words - bring unto HIM, thyself, as a living example; as a living sacrifice: come with clean hands: and bare heart unto HIM, for He knoweth that which is hidden therein.

I say, ye have no secrets; for has HE not created thee? And didst HE not send thee out from HIM a living SOUL? PERFECT AND COMPLETE! I say unto thee - ye children of darkness - ye have deprived thyself of great glory; and ye have forfeited thy rightful inheritance, for thou hast followed the 'dragon' down to perdition and I say, turn from him and seek thy freedom from bondage. And when thou dost cry out with thy whole heart - all thy Soul - all thy power - all thy might! I say unto thee HE, the Father, shall send a legion unto thee; ye shall ask thy freedom of the Father/ Mother God and NO MAN is responsible for thee! Now let it be recorded herein that ye shall WILL thyself free! And ye shall surrender up thy own free will, unto the FATHER, the giver of LIFE; HE, which hast sent thee forth; HE shall not forsake thee - neither shall thou deceive thyself! For therein is great danger! I say unto thee; give unto No man a penny for thy salvation! Yet I say, ye shall give of thyself that ye may receive of HIM, thy own salvation - I too say, ye shall remember thy benefactors; them which have given their life - their ALL, as defenders of the LIGHT; truth; and JUSTICE: them which doth hold the LIGHT that ye may find the way: FORGET THEM NOT.

Be ye mindful of them, for they have walked the path of Light, and lived according to the law - they have earned the right to call themself Sons of God; Abide within the law, and love ye one another; and I shall reveal myself unto thee when thou art prepared to receive me, and of me - I AM thy Older Brother

Sananda - Son of God.

Recorded by Sister Thedra of the Emerald Cross

The Great Day of Judgment

My Beloved: This day has been given us for our part of the GRAND PLAN which we bring forth at this hour; I say at this hour hast thou come that ye may partake of this plan - which we bring forth in <u>this day</u>: The Great Day of Judgment - the Day of Decision; let thy hand be my hand - thy voice My voice - let thy will be my Will; and say unto them as I would say that they shall arise and be about the business at hand! Now let it be said; that when it is come that they are discomforted they shall cry out; and they shall be as ones which hast thrown overboard their own life belt –

Yet I say, that when they turn unto the Light and bear witness of words, which they give so freely (which they say is of God) they shall be as ones heard; for it is the heart which is seen, and which is judged; for as a Man is - So do we see him! We see not that which he THINKS himself: yet he does deceive himself, we thy Sibors, thy benefactors know him for that which he is we see as he sees not; for we are not bound in darkness; neither are we deceived by hollow words. I say when they are as ones contrite of heart - do turn and seek their own salvation of the Father they shall be brought out; and they shall be liberated, and they shall be glad!

Ye shall be as one which has my hand upon thee; and give unto them these MY WORDS - and when they are of a mind to hear ME I shall give unto them a "New Song" sweet beyond ALL words; no pen can pen them; no words of mouth hast spoken them, and their joy shall know no bounds!

Harken unto ME! Ye Children of EARTH! Give unto me credit for being that which I AM; and I shall give unto thee thy gift supreme; I say I shall give unto thee thy 'gift supreme' when thou hast given unto Me credit for that which I AM - and thou hast followed me unto the end. Be ye not so foolish as to think I AM within the world for the sheer folly of it! I KNOW what I AM about; and I AM not sleeping: neither am I from the realms of the 'dead' I AM not of the 'Netherworld' - Neither AM I of the Earth –

I AM from and of the Father, sent of HIM that ye may be brought out of bondage this day! That ye may not be caught napping; that ye may be freed from the wheel of rebirth - that ye may be caught up with lie - I say: "THAT YE MAY BE CAUGHT UP WITH ME" For have I not said that I AM come with a "Host" of MY ANGELS, (if you like) to which have been unto themself true; which have gone the same way I have gone - them which knoweth thee, and thy suffering - torment and anguish. I say they have attained the 'Royal Road' they have gone out - they have returned that ye may attain thy freedom, grant them thy respect, thy love, thy cooperation, that ye may know such joy as they have; that ye too may earn theirs (their respect) - that ye may go where they to - that ye may be blest as they are blest.

I say ye have not known freedom - ye have not earned thy freedom ye shall free thyself - WILL IT SO - and let ME say here that ye do not earn it by raising sword of might - ye gain not thy freedom by MIGHT OF MAN OF EARTH! Neither do ye gain thy freedom by enslaving thy brother - this is thy folly - OH, MAN, NEVER WAS IT SO!

Now ye shall be no part of their foolishness! I say unto them: which are so foolish, thou fool! Knowest that which thou Bindest shall bind thee? I say it is the law - free them! FREE THEM!

Yet ye' shall stand thy ground, and let no man bind thee, with his thinking; his creeds, his dogmas: say unto the Father/ Mother God; "UNTO THEE ALL THE POWER, AND GLORY: HERE I AM, FATHER, DO WITH THIS THY CREATION AS THOU WILL: USE IT TO GLORIFY THYSELF: THAT ALL MEN MAY KNOW THEE THY FREEDOM."

Bless them that which misuse thee; give unto them thy love give not the bitter cup - yet make not a fool of thyself: I say stand thy ground; and keep it holy - do not contaminate it, sanctify it; for thou art the creation of GOD the Father, created of HIM PERFECT! Cleanse thyself and all shall become pure! I say sanctify thyself - and the ground upon which thou standeth shall become HOLY; HEAR ME! OH YE CHILDREN OF EARTH! Give unto me ear, turn this day and follow ye ME, I shall give unto thee peace, and surcease from pain. I am The Wayshower, I AM Sananda.

Recorded by Sister Thedra of the Emerald Cross

Now I Am Returned

Beloved; this day have I spoken unto thee; and I say I am not finished for there is much to be said; and let it be recorded, when I am finished there shall be another day - another place, another part for them which have followed ME; for I say I shall lead them into the Light wherein they shall abide with me. I say they which follow me shall abide within the Light which never fails; wherein there is no sorrow. I say this is the day of decision; wherein have I been found wanting? Have I not kept my covenant with them? Have I not prepared the place for them?

NOW I AM returned unto them; yet they know me not! I say pity are they! For I find them sleeping; and they are as ones sleeping the sleep of the 'dead'. I say unto thee they are a sad lot! Now ye shall be unto them my hands, my voice for this part, and they shall accept them for that which they are, or they shall be caught up short; I say they shall be caught napping.

Now ye shall give unto them this word, and they shall be reminded of these MY WORDS when it is come that they are discomforted and they shall be a one which shall call out LORD! LORD! Hast thou forgotten us? Or, they shall make haste unto ME and prepare themself to receive Me and of Me and they shall be diligent in their search for Me - they shall be unto each other comfort - they shall be mindful of each other - and they shall be as each other's keepers; for it is not given unto man, to stand alone; he has been given fellow brothers that they may have companionship - they he may live as ONE in the SPIRIT OF BROTHERHOOD - of ONE PARENT, sent into the Earth that the Father may be glorified in them –

By them and through them: that HE may be unto them great joy! In turn giving unto HIM joy; for He has sent them forth that they may glorify HIM, and return unto HIM. I say they shall return unto HIM in the fullness of time; yet it is blessed to return this day: for this is the day of salvation. When they shall be given their choice of returning unto HIM as Sons of GOD - of God, or going into utter darkness, and beginning from the beginning! I say unto thee, My Beloved, I know therein is no comfort for the weary and wonton ones, until they lay aside all their rebelliousness, and hatred and ask of the Father forgiveness: and has He denied them?

Yet I say unto them: the day of decision is come - for the time draweth nigh when they shall be forced with the part, which shall call for great and hasty decision for there shall be no time to waste - THERE SHALL BE NO TIME TO WASTE!

For time runs out! and this is the day long-prophesied and they know not it is come - here - NOW! Blame not another - I say unto them for thy frailties; for thou hast heard these my Words - for I am not alone; I say I AM NOT ALONE! I have come with many of my Brothers from the realms of Light, that ye may know that there is a new day - a new dispensation - and new laws now revealed which ye have not known - this is MY DAY! Sayeth the Lord God of Hosts, and I AM HE, I have spoken so be it I shall speak again and again.

I AM, Sananda

Recorded by Sister Thedra

The Greatest Power Upon the Earth

Beloved: Another day, another hour, another part we add unto that of the others; how is that we accomplish this? Through our 'oneness', one with the other; and I say "ONE WITH THE OTHER" now let us say, we are not divided; we are 'one' and as one we have our BEING within the Father/Mother God - manifest in the Earth as people - as MAN! - as Earthlings. Yet I say unto thee, My Beloved, we are not of Earth, we have come from the place wherein HE, our Father abides, none other; for I say we are sent of HIM, and are of HIM, for this have I come, that they who are lost may be found.

I say unto thee, there are ones which have been sent for a purpose which have had their memory blanked from them, and they know not their source - their destination - these I have come to remind, these which call out for their memory - these which do 'will' to return unto their source for I say unto them: The Father has sent ME that ye may return with me - for I shall return when it is come that I have found them who are aware, and who do answer my call: yet let this be recorded that I shall leave on the appointed hour and the doors shall close behind me for this day shall end, as all others have ended and thy waiting shall be filled with anguish! I say thy waiting shall be filled with anguish!

Now be ye as wise as the serpent, and give this 'MY WORD' some thought; meditate upon it; and I say that ye shall prepare thyself for this day; which is NOW COME! And there is no moment more precious than this - for it is the "NOW" ye have - Ye have no promise of the morrow! For it may be that ye be found wanting! Ye are told again and again that this is the day of salvation, so be it and SELAH.

Be ye as one prepared for the greater part; I say the GREATER part for that have ye waited - ye have waited <u>many an age</u>; and what hast thou found in this day? Hast thou found thy waiting profitable? Hast thou found thy freedom from pain, want, misery, of any kind? Hast thou found thy longings all satisfied? Hast thou been unto thyself true? Hast thy memory been restored thee? Wherein have ye been filled with joy and gladness, free from all care, all sorrow? Wherein does thy "FREEDOM" lie? Wherein hast thou found it? Wherein hast thou gone wherein they are free from pain, and sorrow?

I say LOOK at them! Ask of thyself, where are they going? From whence comest they? and myself, from whence comest I?? from WHENCE? I say unto thee: ye dreamers: AWAKEN! ARISE! Alert thyself and come unto ME, and I shall give unto thee GIFTS thou knowest not of! For I shall restore thy memory, and ye shall know that which hast been hidden from thee; and ye shall not be deceived, for ye shall know the TRUTH; and all thy longings shall be satisfied.

And ye shall control the elements - and ye need not grovel for a pittance, for bread, for ye shall command the elements, and the 'thing' commanded shall bring forth the material imaged, into material substance. I say it shall come forth as a finished idea, made manifest; and it shall satisfy thy longing; for it shall be done according to the law unto the WILL of the Father, for ye shall create like unto HIM, by the "Spoken Word" and in HIS NAME shall ye do these things: yet I say unto thee, take HIS name not in vain! Woe to anyone - anyplace which do: for I say this is the GREATEST POWER UPON EARTH! Yea, within the firmaments!

For HE is ALL there is, and NONE OTHER! I say HIS name is power - use it to bless thyself - and ye shall bless others in like manner.

Yet I say, ye shall know that ye have the authority, and the WISDOM to use it - for this shall ye wait, for it is great danger to go into such power unprepared! I say when ye have so prepared thyself I shall disclose the power held within HIS name, and the "WORD" SOLEN AUM SOLEN. Trifle not with it! I AM HE, which knows and I use it not thoughtlessly - I All come that ye may know these laws - Be ye blest for thy fidelity.

I AM Sananda, Son of GOD.

Recorded by Sister Thedra of the Emerald Cross

I Am a Simple Man

My Beloved: I say unto thee this hour, that there is not one of them which has not betrayed themselves at some time - for this are they bound in darkness. Now I say unto them this day; that they have been given a new dispensation wherein they may choose <u>this</u> <u>day</u>, their place wherein they shall go - for <u>GO</u> they shall! For the Earth shall be freed for a time of all living creatures; both animal and man; flying and creeping creatures shall be put into their respective places, and man and animal shall be separated: and put into his own place –

His own atmosphere, his own environment and therein he shall dwell until he learns his lessons well and in of his own will shall he come into his rightful inheritance - When he has tired of his suffering and anguish, he shall call unto his Father for peace and surcease from all torment - I say he shall torment himself until he is at last weary of it: then he shall cry out unto the Father, and then, he shall be heard, -

and answered. And none shall bring him against his own will - that is wisdom for it shall be of his own will that he is brought out of his bondage.

Now let this go on record: that I AM come that they may know the law - yet I come to bring them out, I break not the law: for I say WE, thy Sibors abide by the law; we ask of thee the same! So be it the better part of WISDOM! Now My Beloved: it is better that they know not the law than to break it! Yet, it is my part to enlighten them - and their part to apt themself; and they are accountable for that which they do with mine words, for I say they are sacred, and holy and they shall be as such; for have I not sibored thee well that ye may be prepared for the part of giving these 'MY WORDS' unto them, unadulterated? And have I not given them as I see fit, without any pretense to their "letters" I say I am a simple man –

I speak unto them which have a mind to hear me - and unto them who ask for the "letter" let him have the letter! I come that they may be free! Free, from their dogmas; creeds; bondage; leg irons; and all their hypocrisy which is an abomination in my sight! I say I am not so foolish as to give unto them 'MY PEARLS' without price for they shall be brought low - and they shall come as a little child and they shall see the foolishness of their ways - and they shall stand shorn of all their glory - their VAIN GLORY! They shall say unto the Father/Mother God: "FATHER I COME AS A LITTLE CHILD: DO WITH ME AS YE WILL: I COME - I COME RECEIVE AS THY SON"*

I say this shall he do - yet it shall be language of the heart - not of the lips for NO hypocrisy shall be seen within thy heart - ye shall come clean of heart and hands - and ye shall call out with thy WHOLE HEART! Make not a liar of thyself by thy idle words, and vain repetitions; for they are a mockery in my sight, I say be not so foolish as to deceive thyself - I say bless thyself as ye would be blest - First, and last, BE UNTO THYSELF TRUE! I AM HE, which has come that ye may be brought out before the great day of sorrow! I say follow ye me - I AM, Sananda.

Recorded by Sister Thedra

*This is a joyful surrender.

Give Him Credit

Beloved: Another part I give unto thee and at this moment, I would say unto thee; I am come for the purpose of giving unto thee the "GREATER PART"; yet this shall be done/accomplished ere the 'greater' part: now when it is accomplished/finished, (this part) we shall go into the other part, which is yet to be accomplished after this is finished.

Say unto them; it is now time that they alert themself; and give unto me the credit for being that which I AM - and stir themself; and begin to live the laws, which I have set before them. When it is come, that they are prepared to receive in 'greater' capacity I shall give unto them that which is for them; now it is given unto me to lead them, as sheep yet they are not of a mind to be led: they are rebellious; they have their mind fixed upon the work of the dragon; they seek signs, and wonders, which he doth show them: which doth deceive, and attract them - they run hither and yon, seeking after him - they are not stable; they are blown about by the foul winds - which shall pass, and leave them covered with debris - with the filth in its wake! I say they are not firm in their knowing: they are foolish: they are plundering the works of others - of ages past! They have not the mind to receive of me direct! While I am now here for this purpose, they are looking backward and I say they see not that which is before them.

I say they are walking backward, and they shall fall; and they shall cry out "MY Lord, I am fallen, help thou me!" Then the hand shall lift them up; and again, they shall spit upon 'the hand' which hast lifted them: and they shall give unto themself credit for all their "wisdom" and strength: and I say again they shall fall! And NO hand shall stay them! For 'the hand' shall withhold its mercy; and judgment shall be given in mercy, and righteousness.

I say it is the better part to withhold the help and assistance at times; for they shall learn their lessons well! This is the last day herein this class wherein they may earn their 'Mastership' and when it is accomplished they shall be free: and not until they can earn it shall it be given them: then, I say they shall earn their 'Mastership/ Sonship' and then they can raise the dead; heal the sick by the spoken word: they can fly! without gadgets! - they will BE Masters of the elements - for they shall be free from the attraction of the Moon, and free from the gravitation of the Earth.

I AM free - and as I AM so they shall they become - I say they shall become even as I and that which I have done, they shall do: and I say unto them; it is not apparent that which 'MAN' shall become: for he shall "BECOME" as the Father/Mother God: for this has he waited: for as yet, he has not become as I. And for this have I come, that they may be made clean - and purified, then I shall give unto them that which I have kept for them.

I say unto thee, My Beloved, I have kept the "GREATER PART" for them! Yet I say they shall earn it: they shall earn the right to walk in "My Sandals" to wear "My Cloak" they shall earn the right to the ORB, and the Scepter, which is power and wisdom. I say I AM not so foolish as to give the babes at the breast "My Pearls" which know not their worth; they are as little ones, which know NOT the PRICE! I say they shall come to know ere they finish!

Bless this day; keep it holy - and immaculate - Let not thy foot slip. Hold thy peace and poise be unto thee, My hand rests upon thee, and I say unto thee, ADOMNI SHELOHEIM AMNI SOLOAH.

Recorded by Sister Thedra of the Emerald cross

Gall for Water

My Beloved: I am now come, that I may add another part unto the other parts which have been given thee for them, and it is for them which have a mind to follow me: for they are the ones, which shall give ear and they shall know my voice and follow me; I say weary not of them; for they shall be as ones which have an ear - and they shall hear and turn unto me - they shall endure their suffering so long - then, they shall tire of it, and cry out, and they shall be as ones prepared for to listen to mine words - and listen they shall! For I say they shall be as ones prepared to hear me out: now this seem a little thing unto them; yet what have I said unto them? I say they are not alert! For they have NOT heard that which I have said.

Now I say; I shall give unto them a part which they cannot misinterpret: for this shall they understand! For that which shall come upon them shall be the common denominator - it shall make of all brothers; and they shall sit down together to lick their wounds; for wounds there shall be! I say wounds there shall be! They shall be as ones prepared for this – for I say they shall be as ones prepared for that which shall come upon them, and for this have they waited, they have not been as brothers!

They have tormented each other - they have given each other the 'bitter cup' and they have given the ones which have asked for bread a stone. They have given GALL for water! They have asked for blood to cleanse themself. I say: Behold the HAND of God, moveth! And it is powerful and it is strong. It is just and it is loving - Too, I say none shall revile thee for these 'MY WORDS' for I AM responsible for them!

I see and know that which shall come upon them; I Am come that they may not suffer; yet they wait; they call <u>My Servants</u> foolish - I say unto them they are the foolish ones, and they shall be faced with their foolishness, yet they think themself wise.

Blest are the lowly, and the just, for they shall be brought out. I AM HE, which has MY hand upon thee; I Come that they may know wherein they are staid. I AM Sananda,

"Suffering makes of all men BROTHERS." Sananda.

Recorded by Sister Thedra of the Emerald Cross

SACRED SYMBOLS

Beloved: This is our day; the day I shall give unto thee this part for them which are of a mind to follow me, and I say they alone shall hear my voice and follow me; too, I say, they shall be as ones prepared to enter into the Holy of Holies with Me: for I say, I give not myself unto the wonton and willful for naught, for I AM now come that there may be Light - that the illusion may pass - that they may be free, I say, that freedom might be given them, as it is given me.

Yet My Father has willed them free; they have gone into bondage of their own free will: and not of their OWN shall they seek me out, I AM not in the Earth for naught: It is MY WILL that they follow Me - yet I say they are as yet asleep! Now I say unto them: there are not one of them, which do "think" themself wise, which doth have the fullness of my estate: I say they are not within the place wherein there is no darkness: they are NOT FREE! I say I AM FREE! They go in and out of their council rooms with their fine "Cloaks of Authority" - they wear the symbols of power and wisdom, and understand NOT the meaning thereof; for I say; there is POWER within the symbol, yet, the symbol has NO power: that which they plunder, has NO power: that which is power, is symbolized, by the characters or notes which they have plundered or pilfered!

They have the fortune to be of the 'Goat Mind '* and they think themself wise: they are not of the MIND of GOD: wherein there are NO mysteries. Now let this be recorded: They shall be given the authority to use such sacred symbols when they are so prepared, and they shall wear them with grace and dignity, they shall make no mockery of them; THEY shall be as ones which know the meaning of these holy expressions, expressed in the forms of like manner. I say, they which are of the 'Goat Mind" do not know the meaning of these things which they bedeck themself in - they carry them about as something to show that they might be looked upon in awe; but I say unto thee, My Beloved; never was this intended for these are sacred; these are words which are not spoken; yea, volumes which have not been written! Who can say in words, what the cross is - what it meaneth? Who knows the fullness of the Emerald Cross? Who knows the fullness of the Croux and the Miter –

Who knows these things? Of man of flesh and bone it is NOT revealed! I say I AM the REVELATOR: and I do not betray myself - I do not betray MY TRUST. I AM the GRAND MASTER - and I AM a competent one. I do not waste MY energy on the willful or the wonton, I seek mine sheep, which knoweth mine voice; I say unto them; "FOLLOW THOU ME" Let us make haste, for the day of the Lord is come! And it is so! I come to gather them in, and ye shall be fortuned to be as one of them; blest be this day; great joy shall be thine, I Am thy Sibor - Sananda.

*"Goat Mind" - the Intellectual mind

Recorded by Sister Thedra of the Emerald Cross

The Last Bitter Dreg

Beloved: I come that I may speak unto them, through thee, and my hand make manifest unto them. I say that they which are deaf, and hear me not, shall <u>see</u> that which I say; and they which are blind, shall <u>hear</u> that which I say; and they which are both blind and deaf, shall be brought to sight and hearing; for I shall cause them to see, and to hear; for I shall give unto them a new kind of portion, and they shall have it marked upon their brow; for they shall NOT forget it! I say they shall remember that which they shall be given: for it is that which they have portioned out for themself! Now for the first time, I say unto them; they shall be as one which has given unto himself the bitter cup; yet they shall drink it to the last dreg - THE LAST BITTER DREG!

I say they shall drink their own bitter cup, which they have portioned out for themself - they shall cry out for deliverance: yet there shall be no surcease from pain and sorrow - until they have atoned for all their misused energy; and turned unto the Father for their freedom: I say when they have turned unto HIM, they shall be delivered out! Let not their cup be thine - for thy own shall NOT be theirs - give unto <u>none</u> the bitter cup –

Yet hold out a hand unto them, that they may see within thy own cup, that which I have filled it - so be it that they shall sup with thee, when they are so prepared: for I say there shall be plenty, and to spare, for I say thy cup shall run over - spill over - spill upon them, and they shall be filled with that which spilleth over, I say they shall lap it up, that which doth spill over from thy cup. Let it be so; so be it I am cone that their cup be filled; yet when they do turn it bottom up, and turn from me, I say I shall fill another, abundantly and a surplus, So let it be for thee.

I AM thy Older Brother - Sananda.

Recorded by Sister Thedra of the Emerald Cross

Warning!

Beloved: This day we give unto them this part, and it shall profit them; for it is the part which they have waited; and when they so love each other, that there be no quarrels, no porang (?) between them they shall have great and glorious revelation; yet I say while they do spit upon each other, and revile each other - give each other the bitter cup - and call for their brothers blood then, and only then, shall they have greater revelation.

I say all condemnation shall cease ere it is revealed unto them!

Now it is given unto ME to see them making the part which they shall have tomorrow, and tomorrow they shall be as ones prepared to swallow it - for have they not portioned it out for themself?

Now let this be unto them a lesson: for I Am not a fool! I speak NOT as such! Yet I say that they shall not look upon these clear and simple words as that of a fool! For I say I am not of a mind to be turned away. I speak unto them who are of a mind to hear me; and I can and do speak as I will –

Yet I will to reach them ALL; they will not, to hear Me! Now let this be recorded; that there shall be divers of wars, and rumors of wars; and many shall go down in defeat - and none shall be the VICTORS! NONE shall be the conquerors, NONE shall be the blest! ALL shall be condemned - NONE shall escape the law, and the law shall deal out justice; it shall come quickly; and it shall be as none of their wars! For it shall be ALL the energy which they have misused, and it shall rebound upon them; and all their hatred, malice and preconceived ideas of justice and love, and mercy shall be shattered in the twinkling of an eye!

I SAY THEY SHALL STAND FACE TO FACE WITH THEIR FOOLISHNESS!

I say they shall see the foolishness of the making of instrument of death - speed - war - and their cauldrons of hell - of their great and glorious satellites, and their rockets! For I say their ships of air and sea shall be as toys, and they shall be as bubbles in the air, they shall not work! they shall fail in the end! I say they shall see their handiwork fail them; for this is foreseen by Me, and I AM HE which has given unto them sight and hearing; and yet they put their fingers in their ears that they hear Me not!

I say that they shall stand frozen in their tracks, and they shall say: It is so - IT IS TRUE, WHAT HAS BEEN WRITTEN! For I say it is so; and it shall profit them to heed 'my words' and turn from their wonton and willful ways. I say it is better that they go into the mountains and put themself under the rocks and eat grubs, than to give of their energy unto such foolishness.

I say; be ye not part of it! Sell not thy eternal soul for part of thy own will, which ye have sold unto the dragon, for naught which shall profit thee! He demands thy SOUL! I say he demands thy SOUL! HEAR THOU HE, ye unknowing ones: The dragon, <u>he which was cast down</u>, demands thy SOUL! TURN FROM HIM! I ask of thee naught, be unto THYSELF true, and ask of the Father thy salvation, and ye be delivered, let it so be. I AM sent of the Father that ye be delivered, I stand as one helpless before thee, until thou will that I assist thee, none shall bring thee against thy will.

Yet I say, I do warn thee that thy errors shall cease; for many of My Brothers of Light has been sent even as I - that ye may know the law - it has been given thee in ages past: Yet thou hast not heeded it. Thou hast been warned, and warned again! Yet ye wait, for ye have not heard that which hast been said!

Ye give unto Me no credit for My part; yet I walk amongst thee, and I say ye shall hear Me; for I shall give unto thee a part which thou cannot misinterpret, thou shall stand upon the ground and see My hand move - for I shall unleash all the energy which thou hast misused which is now built up within and around the Earth: and I say great shall be its power!

Now too, I say, (and heed ye this), I shall deliver out each, and every one which is prepared; yet when it is come thou shall call out; "LORD! LORD! HERE I AM, DELIVER ME!" I say unto thee ye shall be as ones which hast betrayed thyself; for I shall withhold Mine mercy - for I say unto thee, this is the day of MERCY! I say let it be so with thee! THIS DAY - CEASE THY FOOLISHNESS! and seek thy salvation of the Father, and for HIS Love and mercy knows no bounds!

Harken unto Me: and I shall hear thee, and I shall show MY hand, and it shall be filled with MERCY! and ye shall not be destroyed.

I AM HE which hast come that ye be delivered out - let it be so.

Yet as thou portion out unto others, so doth thou portion out for thyself - it is the law, hear thou Me, and I shall reveal Myself unto thee.

I Am Sananda, the Nazerine, The Wayshower

Recorded by Sister Thedra, through HIS GRACE.

The Gift of Mind - The Tree of Knowledge

Berean speaking unto thee, on the subject of mind: Now to continue the subject; was it not said that 'mind' is a gift of God the Father, and was it not given unto each and every one which did go out from HIM in the beginning?

Yet they used this great and glorious gift for their own senses and they have degenerated into the lower state called human; and is he not a blight upon the Father's Handiwork?

I say he has brought about his own downfall, he has sought out the dragon - the one cast down! And they have followed him. Now I say that the Father has seen fit to give unto them a new dispensation; and it is now come when they may return into their rightful estate, their original place, wherein they may have all their 'gifts' returned unto them.

Now I say it is expedient, that I say unto them; that they shall give unto HIM all the credit and the glory, and they shall become self-less, that they may become as HE, the Father; for to become as HE, they shall become selfless and they shall be as ONE with HIM.

For He is the giver, and the taker, and He has given unto them being, and unto HIM, all the credit ALL the GLORY!

Now that I have spoken on the preparation for the gift of GODHOOD; I say that MIND is of God; IS GOD; and yet because of thy free-will thou hast gone into darkness; thou hast been as ones which hast had thy memory blanked from thee, for thy transgressions hast been great indeed!

For thou hast betrayed thyself, and thy trust; for thou wast sent forth that thou shoudst glorify the Father in the Earth: yet thou didst go into the dens of iniquity - and thou didst create in thy own image, that which HE did NOT! Thou didst beget like unto the whore!

Perfectly, wast thou created: and imperfect, hast thou created. And I say for this, hast thou had thy memory blanked from thee: yet I say ye shall again eat of the 'TREE of KNOWLEDGE' for it is within thy memory! I say all things are recorded therein: for therein is NO secret therein is the record of TIME: all things are recorded within the 'TREE of KNOWLEDGE'

And I say ye which are so prepared shall eat of the fruit, of the 'TREE of KNOWLEDGE' for this is thy inheritance from the beginning: and were it not so I would not say it: for I Am thy Sibor, and I AM the one sent for this part of thy learning; and ye shall learn this well! For I say it shall not be changed in any manner WHATSOEVER! For therein is thy downfall, ADULTERATION!! thou hast adulterated EVERYTHING: even unto the AIR thou breathest!

Beloved: ye shall come again, and I shall speak unto thee, that they may have Light. I say unto thee, ye shall rest thy pore, for this hour has ended thy labors for the day. I bless thee with my presence; and bless thee with MY BEING: for I AM ONE with the Father/Mother GOD; I say I bless thee with MY BEING, now ye shall bless them as I bless thee I AM Berean.

Recorded by Thedra

Traitors in High Places

Beloved; - Now it is said, and rightly so, that there are 'none so sad as he which betrays himself, or his trust.' Yet thou hast seen not the last of it; for I say, that there are ones which doth sit in high places which have the part of betraying their trust. For I say they have sold the freedom of their fellow countrymen for a 'pence' I say, "FOR A PENCE".

Now let it be recorded herein this script, that there are many true and just within the high places; yet this is as it should be! And they are not to be overlooked; for I say; were it not for them, thy nation would no longer be a Nation of people - white or black; neither brown nor yellow, neither red - for it should be destroyed completely! I say were it not for the just and true ones.

Yet I say there are ones which doth sit in high places which have sold their worth; they have given unto the Dragon great praise! and glorified him. I say they have spoken with a double tongue; forked with three prongs - as it were, for I say they speak in riddles that the people know NOT that which they say. They ask of thee, the sweat of thy brow; and the labor of thy hands - FOR WHAT? I say they have said this; and that; and thou hast forgotten what hast been said; for they talk so loud, and long thou cannot hear them, for I say the ones which have tried, cannot follow their places - I say their places. I say they are as actors which go from scene unto scene - using many parts, which are not convincing which are not as the script; they do not follow the script, shall we say: not in THEIR play - their game!

I say they are playing a losing game, these false one. I say unto thee, they are FALSE! and they are not at peace with themself. I say, too, that they - the false ones - shall find one on which to place <u>his</u>* blame;

for he shall be as one undefended and unprotected, by the world of men. Now let me say it thusly: "ONE!" shall bear the burden of many traitors; for there are more than ye care to know! Not that ye shall not know them; for I say they shall be exposed.

For have I not said that justice shall reign supreme! And all things shall be weighed and balanced? Have I not said that there are none so sad as the one which betrays himself, or his trust? It is SO! Yet the fools that they are, heed not the law, yet they shall be caught up short of their course.

Let it suffice that, each unto his own, and each shall receive as he is prepared; and I say great is the law and swift doth it deal out JUSTICE! Let not thy heart be troubled; for I say that there are ones prepared for that which shall be done: and not one of thy Sibors shall be caught off guard!

Too, has it not been said that this is MY LAND, MY COUNTRY, MY NATION, have I not founded it? Have I not guarded it? Yet I say there shall be trying times: it shall be purged, cleansed, and purified: and I shall set up my banner, and NOTHING, shall prevail against it! I have spoken fearlessly and justly. I say, I shall point them out, ONE by ONE! And ye shall know them.

I AM thy Sibor, Sananda.

*Note the individual's responsibility of 'this' blame

Recorded by Sister Thedra

Love

Berean speaking unto thee -

Beloved: For the purpose of giving unto thee this part, to be added unto the other parts. Now we shall call this part that of "Love" and I say it is the motivating part of life - it is "Life" in its first magnitude: I say 'first magnitude' for that is in its purity, or in the first class - the order in which the Father/Mother conditioned it in the beginning.

Now I say unto thee Love is the motivating interest of the Father/Mother God, it motivates each and every particle which is brought into manifestation: it holds the atoms in bonds - it is the cohesive quality which binds together the atoms - the great bulk of atoms, and even the universe, For I say the universe is an atom, in the mind of GOD; for He has begat more than that which ye know.

I say it is infinitum, that which HE has created; the universes without* and peopled them, he has done even more! Tongue cannot express; no person can convey HIS works, for man is but (as yet) an infant in his place, wherein he finds himself - for it has as yet not become apparent that which he shall become. I say, Man of Earth, shall become even as the Father, for they shall return unto HIM in due season and then, they shall be like unto HIM; and then, they shall know as He knows - and they shall go into darkness no more. Now this shall be after they have prepared themself for their return - and they shall make haste! And it is now come when HE has given unto them a new dispensation; and they shall be given the opportunity to cleanse themself this day and return unto HIM. And for this has HE sent many of HIS Sons, that they may be given the greatest assistance man of Earth has ever had: and that is through HIS mercy and love.

I say he so loved them that he has spared them for this day - He has gone the long way to bless them; He has proven HIS LOVE for them - I say they have turned their face from HIM; HIM - which has given unto them life, and which hast been merciful unto them. Now they deny HIM! And they do believe themself alone! While there are ones which 'profess' HIM, yet they say He is a 'thing' - He is a 'part' - HE IS NOT! and they are as the Babylonians - they are divided, and they babble as fools, knowing not from whence they came, nor whither they goest, I say LOVE hast kept them in the first place; and were it not for HIS love they should all perish.

Yet I say unto them; that they shall turn from their waywardness, and willfulness and return unto HIM ere the time cometh when the hour shall strike, and the gate shall close in their face; for as thou hast portioned out unto thyself, so shall ye receive: and ye shall be dealt with justly. For there are no exceptions! I say there are NO exceptions! Be ye alert - and heed these MY WORDS - Love ye one another - Love ye HIM, which hast given unto thee BEING: give unto HIM thy whole heart, thy WHOLE BEING, and great shall by thy joy.

I AM Berean,

Recorded by Sister Thedra of the Emerald Cross

*Outside our own universe

Charity

Beloved: I come this day to speak on charity: charity, being the first and last aspect of LOVE; for without charity there is no love. I say without charity there is NO love. And it is now come when ye shall give them this part and they shall remember it for without this the other scripts are not complete - I say that the other aspects are but the parts, or aspects of the 'whole' which is love - the WHOLE being LOVE. And love contains all other aspects (laws) included with any, and all aspects given hereto, or henceforth for them to live by.

I say love includes CHARITY, MERCY, and JUSTICE; and are ONE in essence. For without one of these there is no virtue; for one cannot practice one of these so-called 'virtues' without being virtuous, and with one only it is not so: for one virtue cannot divide them, these aspects, into parts; for to be TRULY virtuous, they Do love each other, they ARE merciful; and they ARE just, and they ARE charitable, for and because of these qualities; for it is these qualities which they are! The becoming that which makes them virtuous; and because of this virtue they ARE virtuous!

Now I say without one of these qualities they are NOT virtuous! Be it so, and so be it. Now ye shall say unto them in my name, that there are not one of them which doth profess 'virtue' which ARE; without ALL the qualities. And I say they do deceive themself!

Now let it be said, that when they love each other as themself - they shall be filled with the other aspects; they shall know the foolishness of their wonton (rebelliousness) and willfulness one unto the other; and they shall be as brothers, one unto the other - and they shall bear no hatred one for the other; they shall have no condemnation one for the other - they shall bless the other as they would have ME bless them.

They will go the last mile for the brother which has not these virtues. I say he will be filled with justice and love - and the goodness of his heart shall make of him a charitable person. This is my part for now, on this subject; and give it unto them as I give it unto thee; and say unto them that they shall not deceive themself; for justice shall rule supreme, and they shall come to know wherein they betray themself.

Love ye one another; and that includes even ME, I AM thy Sibor, Berean.

Recorded by Sister Thedra of the Emerald Cross

Spirit

Beloved of My Being: Now it is come when another shall come unto thee for the purpose of giving unto thee a part for them - and this part shall profit them which are of a mind to read, hear, and see and learn. I say they which do see that which is written, and do give credence unto the 'word' shall be made to see and hear; I say they shall be given comprehension, so be it and Selah. Now ye shall receive him, the Lord of Saturn, the mighty and strong, the part which he shall give unto thee for them.

I AM Sananda.

The Saturnian Council of Twelve

Beloved of My Soul - HAIL THEE BELOVED: I Stand before the great throne of justice, wherein is Light and Love, and Wisdom - I speak unto thee of SPIRIT: Spirit IMMORTAL - I say that Spirit is not mortal; neither is mortal Spirit - yet because Spirit IS - so is mortal - for mortal would not be, were it not for Spirit. Mortal is motivated and animated by Spirit, created of the Father Mother God, and it is by HIM that mortal becomes God - and as Spirit shall be made GOD - I say that mortal is as yet not perfect, for mortal is the undeveloped state of 'man' and the Spirit is the perfected state - for this has MAN been less than GOD. Yet in the beginning the Father created him perfect; and he went into darkness of his own free will and forgot his SOURCE, he became contaminated, adulterated and he has wandered in darkness since.

Now it is with the consent and the efforts of the Great Council of Saturn that this new effort shall be crowned with success; for I say, that we, of the Council of Twelve, shall be as Counselors unto the ones which have answered. Now it is with renewed strength and effort that we go into action at this time: for I say unto thee, that it is near time when great stress shall come upon the peoples of all lands - all nations, and they shall be as ones torn and worn from frustration: and I say that there shall be a great wave of Light which shall flood the Earth and none shall stand against it which are of darkness;

I say that great and mighty shall be the force of Light - and nothing shall stand within it (of Darkness). Now I say that the 'move shall be slow - yet the action shall be swift and agonizing! Yet for the good of all mankind shall it be! I say; that man, and his power which shall be unleashed upon him, shall be the recipient of his handiwork - for he shall be as ones which have betrayed himself; and I say the suffering shall be great; yet I say we, the Council of Twelve, are alert and we are at our post without day, or night - which thou knowest: we rest not! For we see and know as ye know NOT! - Now I say ye shall be as one alert and give unto them this part; and it shall go to certain ones which shall be alerted; and I say ye shall stand together as "ONE MAN" for in UNITY there is strength!

And I say: ALL condemnation shall cease! And there shall be unity between them. Let them heed these 'MY WORDS' for I am sent as the spokesman for the Council; and as ye prepare thyself so shall ye receive.

I say unto them; the day quickly approaches when they shall be glad for MY WORDS, and ALL assistance which we are prepared to render unto them. Yet I say that they shall be as ones found trust-worthy, and as they are prepared so shall they receive. I say, that I am now prepared to stand with thee - art thou prepared to stand with us, thy Brothers of the Council of Twelve; whose headquarters are within the great white mountain retreat (SHASTA) I say I am not afar off - and too, I say the day draws near when this retreat shall open its doors unto the ones so prepared, and I too say that there are none so foolish as the ones which betrays himself, and it is given unto me to know! I am with thee; art thou with ME? I ask of thee?! I AM the Saturnian.

Sortuno.

Recorded by Sister Thedra of the Emerald Cross

Silence

Beloved: I come this day that ye may have this part added unto the others for them! To them which do accept these my words and take them unto themself, I say, BLEST SHALL HE BE!

I AM Berean, and I come for the good of all mankind - let it be so. I say that this part shall be called "Silence" and it is NOT one of the lesser virtues for it is the greater part of WISDOM! - Which includes ALL virtues, all virtue. I say that in the silence much of wisdom is revealed unto thee, and when the VOICE is heard in the silence it is louder than the spoken word - for the spoken word only reaches the outer ear; while the unspoken word within the SILENCE reaches the inner ear, the heart, not to be forgotten.

Now I say unto the one which has presented himself upon the 'path of initiation, or attainment' BE YE SILENT OF THY ATTAINI-IENT: let thy work be unto them thy testimony; look not for credit; or glory; boast not of thy attainment; for I say it is a place wherein ye may stumble and fall, and ye may be as one unprepared!

And I say that ye shall learn the WISDOM OF SILENCE!

Ye shall carry NO TALES, one between the other, ye shall be mindful of the laws given unto thee; ye shall give none the bitter cup, portion it not out for thy own self; for have I not said ye shall drink to the last bitter dreg??

I say watch thy words: every last word! Weigh it well! and know it shall return unto thee as the boomerang!!

I say it shall return unto thee either for well or woe; let it be for well; for I say it shall return bearing the likeness of thy own creation a thousand fold.

I say that silence is the better part of WISDOM. Now ye shall remember this; and be ye as ones warned, for I say ye shall withstand all temptations, ere ye proceed upon the path of attainment.

Now ye shall be as one reminded of these MY WORDS; for I say unto thee, there are many pitfalls on the path - and the tongue is the GREATEST of them all! I say that thy own tongue shall be disciplined! And it shall OBEY thy WILL; for it is thine, and as a child it shall obey thy command! Now ye shall. WILL it so!

Now I say, thy frailties are many, yet this one is frailest of them all; let not thy own waywardness trip thee up! I speak for thy own sake; for it is for thy learning that I have come unto this mine servant, and I say for her preparation shall she be blest, and because, of her preparation I am enabled to speak unto thee, be ye mindful of this: I say be ye mindful of this!

I am within the place wherein are no secrets; I see and I know that which ye do, every thought, every word; I say ye have NO secrets, for there are NO secrets in the realm of GOD - wherein there is NO darkness; the darkness lies within thy unknowing: for thy memory has been blanked from thee, and ye are walking in darkness: thou hast forfeited thy gift of memory –

Yet ye shall be given the opportunity to earn it back: ye shall redeem thy forfeit. For I say ye have been given a new dispensation; and a new day; a new law shall be revealed unto thee. For I say ye are NO LONGER under the OLD LAW, for it is now come when many from the realms of Light have come into thy midst that ye may know the TRUTH. I say ye have NOT known the TRUTH; therefore thou art in darkness.

I AM thy Brother, Berean.

Great Light

Beloved; I come this day, for their sake, that they may have these my words; and it shall profit them to take them unto their heart, and remember them; for I say it is now come when there shall be great Light flood the Earth and ye shall witness this my verity unto thee for it is NOW come! I say that great LIGHT shall flood the Earth, and nothing shall stand which doth oppose it.

I come that all may be prepared for the day which is now come - let this be recorded; that when they are discomforted then, they shall cry out for help: yet I say that as a great tidal wave shall they (and all who are caught within it shall feel its power; the power thereof shall be so powerful,) they which have not prepared themself shall perish in the wake thereof.

I say those who have builded their foundations upon quicksand shall be swept before it, and they shall call out; yet I say that they shall be as ones found wanting! THIS is the DAY OF THE LORD! This is the day for which they have waited, and I say that when the thunders roll and the rains come, is no time to begin thy building - yet I say they are hesitant to accept that which has been offered unto them in love and mercy.

For they have been bound by the dragon for many an age - and they have carried with them their leg-irons, and their bondage: while we, thy Brothers of Light come to give unto them the laws and to enlighten them, they turn unto the dragon for security, they ask of others bound in darkness, for their freedom! They do seek in dark places for their freedom - for Light - yet I say they shall find none in such places - for it is not there; were it so they would not be in darkness, they would not be bound.

I say that they who do sit in high places and say: look here, look there, for thy freedom knoweth not the law; they are bound also. Now let us consider, that were they free would they be bound by the same bounds, I ask of thee?

Now I say unto them, that within the realms of Light all things are known: and I say that within the realms of Light lies thy freedom. And thy freedom is assured thee when, ye turn from the dragon (which has held thee) and ye do ask of the Father which hast given unto thee life. I say that thy freedom shall be given unto thee of HIM, as part of thy inheritance. Yet I say too, that thy inheritance shall be given unto thee in full when thou art so prepared to receive it. Then, and only then, shalt thou be free-forever free!

And I say unto thee we, thy Brothers from out the realms of Light, have come into thy midst - that ye may awaken into thy rightful estate.

I say unto thee: ye have been given a new dispensation whereby ye may be released from thy bondage forever: for this do we speak so freely now, at this time. I say unto thee there are many which have come into the Earth even as thy Lord Sananda, who walks the Earth as man; and who has a body flesh even as thou, that this deliverance may be accomplished this day - ere the great day of sorrow!

Now let this be said; that when thou art prepared thou shalt be delivered out: this I repeat again and again! AS THOU ART PREPARED SO SHALL YE RECEIVE" - It is so, so be it, and it is the law! I say so; and that is my part to give unto thee the law of preparation and after thy preparation greater things shall be given unto thee; for this dost thou wait. I AM, thy OLDER Brother, Berean.

Recorded by Sister Thedra of the Emerald Cross

Mind

Beloved: I speak unto thee this day of "Mind" - let thy mind be the mind of GOD the FATHER - pure - unadulterated; keep thy mind staid on HIM, and HIS mercy and grace. I say be ye at Peace and Poise; and bless them, as HE has blest thee; create not chaos for thyself by thy thinking - KNOW that thou are within the palm of HIS hand and be at rest.

I say PEACE - PEACE: Bless them with thy PEACE; Let them sip from thy chalice, of thy nectar; be ye a comfort unto them, and ask of them naught; save obedience unto the law; let thine heart overflow with joy - for HIS GRACE and MERCY - ask for them PEACE; yet Be at PEACE before thou asketh for PEACE for another!

For I say; ye shall first establish PEACE within thyself; and then, ye shall share thy peace with them who knoweth NOT such PEACE! I say ye shall be as one blest; so be it and SELAH.

Now I say MIND is a gift of God the Father; yet ye shall be as one GIFTED of HIM; and ye shall use that gift to glorify HIM, the Father, upon the Earth, that they may come to know HIM, and HIS mercy and goodness; for this hast HE sent thee out. I say HE has given unto thee a gift and it shall be for the good of all mankind!

Now I say let thy mind be the MIND which is of GOD: Let HIS MIND be the mind which is thine; and give unto HIM credit for giving unto thee being: walk ye in HIS LIGHT, and be unto them a lamp by which they shall find their way.

I say that they may walk by thy Light: Now let this be recorded; that they shall see thy Light, and follow it; for this hast thou been sibored.

Now ye shall be as one prepared for the greater part; and I say ye shall not want, neither shall ye falter.

I AM COME that ye may be free from all bondage: Let it be so; So shall it be.

I AM THY Brother, Sananda.

Recorded by Sister Thedra of the Emerald Cross

Purity

Beloved: - While it is now come, and we are about it, let us give unto them this part; Let us call it "Purity": and with this, let us begin with a pure heart - while the other things shall become pure - let us consider the HEART; I say that the heart is the 'chalice' from which they shall drink of the love which shall flow from thine own chalice - which shall spill over, and that, chalice shall be full - from the fount of eternal love which shall flow from the source; so be it and SELAH. I say, that their capacity shall be increased, and they shall be filled and they shall be mindful of thee - for I say they have not known thee; neither have they comprehended thy part: yet I say they shall come to know. Now I say they shall not hold thee accountable for these MY WORDS, yet, I say they shall be held accountable for that which they do with them; they shall hold these words sacred, and not defile them, for they are MINE! And I say, they are valid - and none shall invalidate them.

Now while it is time, I say, unto them; that when the heart is pure, therein is no hatred, malice, bigotry, hypocrisy! And the 'ego' is not self-centered, it is the eternal part which is ever expressing in form - UNTIL it returns unto its dwelling place and is formless, and becomes ONE with the ALL.

And I say that the ego becomes purified throughout the ages and effort of one called 'man' and he finds no surcease from pain and suffering until he has become purified and returned unto his abiding place. Now ye shall be as one prepared for I say unto thee ye shall return this day; and I see and know, I say unto thee, my beloved, thy waiting shall end.

Now ye shall add this part to all the other parts; and they shall have them as My testimony; for I say that there shall be none entering into the place of MY abode with an unclean heart - and I say that their hatred, their sorry ways, shall end! And they shall purify themself; for NONE other shall do it for them! Now ye shall return unto the altar at the hour of thy guests coming; and ye shall commune one with the other, and ye shall be unto her my hand and my foot.

I AM thy Brother Bor.

Recorded by Sister Thedra of the Emerald Cross

Its Long Prophesied

Mighty is the word - great is the power thereof; Beloved: I say unto thee this day that the word shall be made manifest in all the lands of the Earth: for I have sent out Mine HOST, and I say that they shall be as ONES prepared to receive of the HOST, great and powerful manifestations: for therein is the fruit of thy labor.

I say the fruit of thy labor shall be the manifestation of the word and it shall be made manifest in all the lands, unto all the peoples! And I say it shall bring forth the harvest which has long been prophesied. For I say it is now come when a great wave of Light shall come upon the Earth, and great shall be the power thereof, yet I say unto thee my Beloved, some shall go into yet other realms knowing not it is come, they shall go into other realms yet filled with their preconceived ideas of ME, and about ME; and they shall be as ones unprepared!

And these, shall wait for another day when they shall be as prepared for the New DAY! YET ANOTHER DAY; for I say they have waited for this day: now that it is come they still WAIT! WHY? WHAT DO THEY SEEK? SIGNS AND WONDERS? -MIRACLES??

I say unto them, they are as children knowing not that this is the time for awakening! I say, ARISE! Cleanse thyself, and be ye about the Fathers business - and great shall be thy revelation, too, I say: ye have slept through many DAYS, while thy waiting has been long and painful, it shall end, and thy joy shall know no bounds; so be ye as ones which has prepared thyself for none other can do it for thee.

For there is NO vicarious atonement; and when ye are so prepared ye shall be brought out of bondage forever. I say ye shall be brought out of bondage forever! I Am thy Elder Brother which has come that ye may know the law, and have assistance: yet ye shall prepare thyself to receive us, and of us, thy brothers of Light.

For I say We are sent as the HOST, which has come with HIM, the King of KINGS; and I say we have come according unto the scriptures, and that it may be filled according unto the law; and at the command of the Father/Mother God, have we come that it may be accomplished too, I say, all which are prepared shall be caught up with the host; and they shall be free - forever free!

So be it the Fathers will, that all be brought out: yet I say unto the sleepers, ALERT thyself, and give unto ME credit for that which I AM, and give unto ME credit for knowing that which I say unto thee - for I know! While thou art asleep, and know NOT!

I say thou art living in a dream; thou art troubled because of thy dreams: thou art living in the world of illusion! I speak unto thee that thy illusions may pass - Now I say seek thy salvation in, through, and of the Father/Mother God, and it shall not be denied thee.

I Am thy Elder Brother, I have gone before thee to prepare the way before thee.

I AM Sananda.

Recorded by Sister Thedra of the Emerald Cross

Sorrow

Beloved: I come that we may give unto them this part; let us call it "Sorrow". Now when it is fortuned unto them to tear themself away from the Love which holds them within the Light - therein, begins their sorrow; for the way of the transgressor is hard! Will that ye return unto thy rightful place as a Son of God the Father - and all thy sorrows shall cease; for I say that thy joy shall be great!

Now while we are speaking of sorrow, let it be said, that they only sorrow that the ones returned unto their rightful estate have is the sorrow of the brother in darkness: for this do we suffer; for their wonton, and willfulness; for this do we sorrow; for this have we come into the Earth as one of them, that they may have the law, which shall be a lamp unto their feet: I say that WE may be a lamp unto them.

I say WE live the law which we give or bring unto them; for I say that we ask naught other than obedience unto the law; I say we ask of them naught, other than obedience unto the law.

Now I say that they shall live the law; for we come that they may know that which shall profit them: I say they shall profit by the 'New Age' revelation; and they shall be as ones blest to hear, heed and respond unto that which we say unto them.

Now it is come when their sorrow shall be increased, for them which walketh in darkness; I say that they shall be as ones which shall suffer much - yet too, I say unto them ere it is come, turn from thy own wonton (rebelliousness) TURN! TURN! and seek the Light, which never fails; for I say it is the better part of wisdom that ye spare thyself all the torment.

Now I say, ye have the opportunity this day to transmute all thy misused energy and turn unto the Father, THIS DAY! And it is the plan which HE has brought forth - that WE thy Brothers of Light bring unto thee, (the Light - the Law) and give it unto thee; that which thou art prepared to receive: and ye shall prepare thyself for the greater part.

Now ye shall make haste; for I say that great sorrow shall come upon the Earth, and no man shall stay the hand of GOD the Father, for HE, has willed that all the darkness be swept away, for this hast He sent US; now when it is come, ye shall be as ones prepared to go before the winds - or ye shall remain to be consumed thereby.

I speak unto thee, that ye may be spared - for this do I reveal myself, for this have I prepared this one, who is My hand made manifest unto thee. I now speak unto thee through her, that ye may have these MY WORDS: yet ye shall not hold her responsible for them; for they art mine! MY WORDS, and I know whereof I speak I say I KNOW! For there is NO darkness within the place wherein I am - and I am sent to awaken thee.

Now let this be recorded, that when ye so will to follow the Light and to be delivered for the good of all mankind, so shall it be; yet all thy selfishness, thy willfulness, thy wonton, all thy condemnation, all thy hypocrisy, all thy bigotry shall be purchased at a price; ye shall transmute it with unselfish love and service to all mankind - ye shall love each other, and every living creature, even as thyself - ye shall bless them even as thou would be blest of the Father/Mother God.

I say bless LIFE - I say BLESS LIFE - be ye grateful for it: for it is GOD, in ACTION! Love freest thou - hatred bindeth thee fast. Bless thyself with thy knowing, and bless thyself with thy action, for this is the day of action. No longer shall ye stand still: for I say ye move; or ye stay within the darkness and become one with it, and it is said; 'the darkness shall be consumed' - darkness shall consume itself, and be no more!

For I say Light shall flood the Earth, and NOTHING unlike it shall remain upon the Earth; nor shall it ever again become part of it, for the Earth shall be delivered out also; she too cries out for deliverance, and it is now being accomplished, and ye shall see it with thine own natural eyes; when thou art of a mind to look.

I say BEHOLD, the hand of GOD! moveth upon the land - upon the sea - in the firmaments of the heavens, yet thou art not of a mind to see!

I say ye shall see it for it shall become apparent unto thee. I AM Thy Brother which is sent that ye may be made to see, and to come into the Light. I AM Berean.

Recorded by Sister Thedra, of the Emerald Cross

Loyalty

Beloved: It is now come when we shall give unto them another part, and this part shall be called LOYALTY, and they shall be as ones which shall remember that which I say; for I say I am aware of thy frailties and I know that they are mindful of their own torment, yet I know wherein thy strength lies, wherein they are staid.

And I say they are now come into the place wherein they shall choose this day which way they shall go; and they shall not deceive themself, for therein is the greatest of folly!

Now let this be recorded that when they give unto the Father their whole heart; their hand, their will, they shall be as ones blest of HIM, and by HIM. Yet they shall not betray themself; neither shall they betray their brother; for to try is to betray thyself.

Now I speak unto the one so foolish, as to try; for I say he which tries to betray his brother ONLY betrays himself. And he which has to account for his own foolishness, SHALL ACCOUNT FOR HIS FOOLISHNESS! I say he shall be the fool and not his brother!

Now I say: that when one says that he has given his brother a farthing and it is not so, it is of little account to thee - yet I say that the law is just, and it is exacting; and it shall be according unto his WORD, he shall come to fulfill his word, even though he has not given the farthing; for I say his WORD shall be made manifest unto the letter for it is now come when they shall see the spoken word made manifest before them. Yet I say we shall see the spoken word made manifest before them. Yet I say we shall make haste to record this, that they may know the law that he which does use it for his own end shall be as one which betrays himself. For any energy which is misused shall rebound upon him, and great shall be the suffering thereof.

Now let this be recorded; that when he has given unto his brother his word, and he cares not for it: speaks carelessly, and for the frivolity of it he is the foolish ONE! Now ye shall remember that when once thou hast spoken a word it goes out, taking form, and returning unto thee -either for weal or woe: and ye shall be aware of the law at all time, and give not thyself the bitter cup - and unto thyself be true. I shall speak again on the subject

I Am, thy Sibor, thy Brother Bor.

Recorded by Sister Thedra of the Emerald Cross

Waiting

Beloved: This day we shall give unto them this part, and it shall profit them, when they have the mind to apply this MY WORD unto themself, and to follow the law which I set before them; for I say none other shall atone for their misused energy - none other comes into their place, for I say, their place becomes theirs when they fill it, none other: I say a place is kept for them, and it remains vacant, until they come to fill it. Be it a glad day when they ALL return unto their abiding place: BE IT A GLAD DAY!

Now I say that we shall call this part, the part of 'waiting' and it shall be the part for which they have waited, and I say it shall. end in due time, when they have prepared themself; I am come that they be prepared - such is my mission to assist them, to bring them unto Light and Understanding of the law –

I say that the law shall be applied unto themself not to or for another; there is not one without exception which comes unto the Father without SELF-preparation, and that is the law, without his own effort! And he shall apply himself to his own preparation, and the law unto his own self, and his own strength and energy shall be applied unto his preparation.

Now they have asked: "HOW DO I PREPARE MYSELF?" I have given the law as simple as language permits: Now I say apply it unto thy daily life and unto all thy ways, all thy doings, dealings, yea, unto thy very life! Expand thy knowledge of the law, by living it to the letter then greater things shall be revealed unto thee, laws hither to shall be revealed unto thee - and MIGHTY shall be the power thereof: yet ye shall be prepared for this revelation, found trustworthy to be entrusted with such power: and ye shall be found trustworthy when this power is revealed unto thee; for it is given unto us thy Brothers of Light to see and know thee - and WE are not deceived!

Now I say when thou hast so prepared thyself, thy waiting shall end; and ye shall be glad: for ye wait that ye may become trustworthy and prepared for the next part. Now let me ask of thee one thing! Art thou obedient unto ALL the laws which hast been given unto thee? Hast thou cleansed out thy own closet; hast thou been true unto thyself? Hast thou condemned thy brother for thy own shortcomings? Hast thou blamed him for thy own foolishness? Hast thou purified thy own self? Hast thou controlled thy own ego? Hast thou disciplined it? Hast thou mastered all thy own faults and shortcomings?

I ask of thee nothing more - I say be ye true unto thyself, and no man shall be unto thee a cross: be ye as wise as the serpent and silent as the sphinx and hasten this day to correct thy own faults, and make straight the way for Me the Lord thy God,

I AM come. - Sananda

Recorded by Sister Thedra

Let Us Consider The Spoken Word

The Lord thy God speaks this day: and MIGHTY is the 'Word' and great the power thereof! I say: Great is the power of the 'Word' and I say the energy which is used in the 'Word' shall be manifest within the world of the seen - let us consider the 'Word' the spoken word - When it leaves thy mouth it goes out as energy, creative energy; and it creates unto its likeness.

When thou givest the energy, power, by the spoken word, it begins its work, NOW! the instant, it is formed into sound it goes out upon the Earth and gathers unto itself its nature, the likeness of itself, and it goes, it goes, until it has spent itself and returned unto its place of birth, as the birds of the air, thy spoken words come or return unto their roosting place: I say they return unto the place from whence they went forth. I say, they return unto thee bearing fruit of the vine; like unto its nature; yet increased a thousand fold.

Now it is said ye shall watch thy words: every single word! They shall be weighed; and weighed again and AGAIN! before it leaves thy lips. It shall return unto thee for weal or woe.

Now let us consider well the Law; for it is given unto thee to know the law - and I say, none shall deny the truth thereof: for the day is now come when ye shall see the fruits of thy words made manifest before thine own eyes: Yea, I say unto thee, they shall be made manifest before thine eyes before they are gone from thy lips!

Now heed well mine words; for the day is now come when the ACTION of the LAW shall be swift; and great the power thereof!

Now ye shall be as ones alert, and give unto ME credit for knowing what which I say unto thee; and for knowing the law! For I AM sent of the Father, that ye too, may know, even as I know - for I say unto thee, the truth, applied, shall profit thee! For ye shall find therein thy freedom from bondage.

I say KNOW THE TRUTH, and it shall free thee from all bondage; when ye so will it. I say WILL, to be free! And by the APPLICATION of the law, ye shall free thyself: yet ye shall apply it unto thyself; for to know and without application, there is no profit.

What should it profit thee to know there is bread, wouldst thou not reach and eat thereof? I say unto thee none eateth of the bread, for thee eat thereof and be filled! I say ye shall will thy freedom by the APPLICATION of the law, and therein is wisdom and ye shall be reminded of those MINE WORDS: Heed them WELL! And be unto thyself true; for I say I give them unto thee out the fullness of mine Love. And I say it is for thy own sake that I speak unto thee.

Be ye blest of me, and by me, I AM Sananda.

Recorded by Sister Thedra of the Emerald Cross

Mission Statement

Give the truth to the world. Let it be received where it will. Many will read the messages. Some will accept the truth, others will read through curiosity, a few will ridicule. Yet to all is the truth given, and to all remains the power of choice.

The hope of the world in these times is in spiritualizing all forms of activity---promoting understanding through love and service. These must be the watchwords if the world is to come into lasting peace. We are trying to influence a world that is going astray and could cause undreamed of suffering. We are trying to overcome the thought of materialists and to bring a spiritual outlook into the earthly life. We need the help of all on earth who can think in spiritual terms. The great battle to be fought now is between the spiritual and the material, between idealism and carnalism. You can help by spreading the word---we are asking that you help because the battle may be long and the victory far away.

Halls of Light is not allied with any sect, denomination, political entity, organization, neither endorses nor opposes any cause. There are no dues for membership. Halls of Light is self-supporting through its own voluntary contributions. Halls of Light has but one purpose: to help through encouragement and understanding...

To contact the publishers or to obtain copies of our other books, please contact us at email: goldtown11@gmail.com

Sananda's Appearance

Be ye as one which hast heard Mine Voice and responded unto it - for I speak that ye hear, and I say that which is wise and prudent.

Let it be known that 1, the Lord thy God hast spoken and bear ye witness of Me, for I have made manifest Mineself that ye might know Me - and for this wast these manifestations made.

I say that I have made Mineself manifest that ye might see Me with thine mortal eyes; that ye might bear witness of Me. Yet thine companions saw and believed not; neither did they hear, for they were selfish and unprepared - yet, did I deny them?

I say; I came that they which would might see and hear. I went and came again unto Mine own. So be it that I have found; I have given unto the found that they which know not might know; that they might come to know as thou knowest.

Yet, how many hast turned from Me and persecuted thee for Mine Word. It is said, "Woe unto them which persecute Mine servants." is it not the law which they set into motion?

Yea Mine beloved, I say they bring about their own downfall. So be it that I am a compassionate one, and I would that they know what they do. So be it they shall learn well their lessons. So let it be, for this is the mercy of God, the One which hast sent Me.

So be it. I AM The Wayshower, the Lord thy God

I AM Sananda

Authority to Use the Name Sananda

Sori Sori: Mine hand I have placed upon thine head, and I have given unto thee the authority to use Mine name. For I first showed Mineself unto thee with the Word: "Go feed Mine sheep. Give unto them the name Sananda, by which they shall know Me as the Lord thy God - the Son of God sent that ye be made to know Me - the One sent from out the Inner Temple that there be Light in the world of men."

Now it is come when ones which have the will to follow Me shall come to know Me by that name which I commanded thee to give unto the world as Mine "New Name." There are many which shall call upon the name of Jesus, yet they will deny the New Name as they are want to do. While unto thee I give assurance that I am the One sent that there be Light in the world of men. Now let this be understood, that they which deny Mine New Name deny Me by any name. So be it I have appointed thee Mine spokesman; I've given unto thee the power and authority to speak for being that which I AM. And I say unto thee Mine child whom I have called forth and anointed thee with the Holy Spirit, thy name shall be as it is now called, Thedra - that name I spoke unto thee from out the eth, and thou heard Me and accepted that which I gave unto thee; and wherein have I deceived thee? Wherein have i forgotten thee, or left thee alone?

I say unto thee, Mine hand is upon thee and I shall sustain thee and ye shall come to know that which I have kept for thee. So be it that I have kept thy reward, and at no time shall it be dissipated or scattered, for it is intact. So let this Mine Word suffice them which question thee - let them question, and I shall bear witness for thee. For do I not know Mine servants from the traitor? Do I not reward Mine servants according unto their works or merits? I speak that they might know that I am mindful of mine servants, that I am not a poor puny priest who hast forgotten his servants.

I say unto them, Mine servants shall be glorified above the crowned heads of the nations which have set themselves apart, and denied Me Mine part of Mine Word - for they have turned from Me in their conceit and forgetfulness.

Now let this go on record as Mine Word, and I shall give unto them proof, which are of a mind to follow Me. So be it I have spoken and I am not finished; I shall speak again and again, and I shall raise Mine Voice against them which set foot against Mine servants, and they shall be as ones cast out. So let them ask of Me and I shall enlighten them. So be it I know whereof I speak. Be ye as ones blest to accept Me and know Me for that which I AM.

Sananda

About the Late Sister Thedra

Since the later part of the last Century the Kumara wisdom preserved by Aramu Muru has begun to reemerge into the world. This process began with the late Sister Thedra, whom Jesus Christ appeared physically to while on her deathbed and spontaneously healed her of cancer while she was in the Yucatan, where she had gone to accept her fate, and the will of our Lord Jesus Christ.

That is when something miraculous occurred. Jesus spoke to her saying, "My name is Esu Sananda Kumara" and then sent Thedra down to the Monastery of the Seven Rays to learn the Kumara wisdom. After five years, Thedra was told to return to the United States where she founded the Association of Sananda and Sanat Kumara at Mt. Shasta in California.

While heading this organization, Thedra channeled many messages from Sananda and taught the Kumara wisdom until her passing in 1992. While in the Yucatan it is said that while Sister during the 1960s Thedra was in the Yucatan, she was told a secret by her friend George Hunt Williamson, also known as Brother Philip, who authored Secrets of the Andes, and the SECRET PLACES OF THE LION.

Williamson, confided in his long-time friend Sister Thedra that he intentionally scrambled the reincarnational lineages in order to protect this next generation when they the Mayan Solar Priests, who were the direct line descendants of the Kumara according to prophesy were scheduled to reincarnate or return to fulfill their missions upon Earth, one of which was to relocate these ancient sites where the original records of the Amaru were placed for safe keeping.

Sister Thedra, 1900-1992, spent five years at the abbey undergoing intensive spiritual training and initiations. While in South America in the Yucatan, she had an experience which changed her in an instant when as it is told by her that Jesus Christ physically appeared to her and spontaneously cured her of cancer.

He introduced himself to her by his true, name, "Sananda Kumara," thereby revealing his affiliation with the Venusian founders of the Great Solar Brotherhoods. It was by his command that Sister Thedra went to Peru where in here travels she met Williamson.

Sister Thedra eventually left Peru upon telling her experience there was complete. Even before she returned to the States she met with harsh criticism from the church, which she elected to leave. She then traveled to Mt. Shasta in California and founded the Association of Sananda and Sanat Kumara. A.S.S.K.

You ask, Is There A Difference Between Jesus and Sananda? Our Lords name given at birth by his Father Joseph, and his beloved mother Mary was Yeshua, thus being of the house of David and the order of Yoseph, he would be called Yeshua ben Yoseph. The Roman Emperors placed the name of Jesus upon the sir name of Yeshua, after the Emperor Justinian adopted Christianity as the official faith of Rome, and ordered that the sacred books be compiled, upon approval of a specially appointed council, appointed by the Emperor, into a recognizable and uniform work titled The Bible. Prior to this there never was a Bible per se.

There existed until the time of the Emperor's edict, a selection of many Sacred texts, that were employed in the Sacred Teachings. Many of which were copies of what the Greeks had transposed from the original texts in the Libraries of Alexandria, which were originally compiled by Alexander the Great, and were destroyed by Julius Caesar, fearing that they might prove dangerous to the rule of a Caesar, an Earthly God.

In addition, it kept. (he thought) the knowledge of Alexander's Libraries, out of the hands of the Ptolemy's, who were said to be descended from his bloodline. At the time Caesar had no way of knowing the vast portions of the Library that were already in the Americas, in the Great Universities of the Inca, and the Maya. Yeshua spent many years in the East after his ascension. The good Sheppard, upon his appearances to the Apostles after his ascension told his Apostles that he was in fact going to tend to his Father's other sheep; which means, plainly that he was continuing upon his sacred journey. As the ascended one, Yeshua took to himself the name of Sananda, meaning the Christed one, and Sananda was thus embraced forever more by the Great Solar Brotherhood. To many of you this is all new, to others it will be received as a welcome easing of the wall that has so long separated two sides of the same coin, this is being placed into the ethers and the matrix of thought at this time as it is the time of the Awakening, and the Christos is already emerging into the new consciousness, and mother Earth herself. Sister Thedra and the phenomenon of channeling.

Authority to use the name of Sananda was given to Sister Thedra when Jesus~ Sananda appeared to her in the Yucatan, and cured her instantly of the cancer that had taken her body over. Further, he allowed a picture of his countenance to be taken at that time that she might realize the occurrence was more than a dream. Thedra had a large format camera called a 620 and it had bellows on it and founded out. She used this to take the picture of Sananda.

Sanada's Message to her by Sister Thedra. "Sori Sori: Mine hand I have placed upon thine head, and I have given unto thee the authority to use Mine name. Give unto them the name Sananda, by which they shall know Me as the Lord thy God - the Son of God, sent that ye be made to know me, the One sent from out the inner temple that there be Light in the world of men." Now it is come when ones which have the will to follow Me shall come to know Me by that name which I commanded thee to give unto the world as Mine "New name."

There are many that shall call upon the name of Jesus, yet, they will deny the new name as they are want to do. While unto thee I give assurance that I am the One sent that there be Light in the world of men. Now let this be understood, that they that deny Mine New Name deny Me by any name. So be it I have appointed thee Mine spokesman; I've given unto thee the power and authority to speak for being that which I AM. And I say unto thee Mine child whom I have called forth and anointed thee with the Holy Spirit, thy name shall be as it is now called, Thedra - that name I spoke unto thee from out the ethers, and thou heard Me and accepted that which I gave unto thee; and wherein have I deceived thee? Wherein have I forgotten thee, or left thee alone?"

"I say unto thee, Mine hand is upon thee and I shall sustain thee and you shall come to know that which I have kept for thee. So be it that I have kept thy reward, and at no time shall it be dissipated of scattered, for it is intact. So let this Mine Word suffice them which question thee - let them question, and I shall bear witness for thee. For do I not know Mine servants from the traitor? Do I not reward Mine servants according unto their works or merits? I speak that they might know that I am mindful of Mine servants, that I am not a poor puny priest who has forgotten his servants."

"I say unto them, Mine servants shall be glorified above the crowned heads of the nations which have set themselves apart, and denied Me Mine part of Mine word for they have turned from Me in their conceit and forgetfulness." "Now let this go on record as Mine Word, and I shall give unto them proof, which are of a mind to follow Me. So be it as I have spoken and I am not finished; I shall speak again and again, and I shall rise Mine Voice against them which set foot against Mine servants, and they shall be as ones cast out. So let them ask of Me and I shall enlighten them. So be it I know where of I speak. Be ye as ones blest to accept Me and know Me for that which I AM. The Final Messages on Saturday, June 13, 1992, at exactly 10.00 PM, at the age of 92, Sister Thedra made her final transition from the comfort of her own bed. When the time arrived, she simply took one small breath and slipped quietly away, without pomp or fanfare.

She left as she had lived...as a humble servant for the greater good. The messages that follow were given to Sister Thedra shortly before her transition. They are compiled here to give you some idea of the significance of her passing and of the expansion of the work, as she is now free to work unencumbered by the physical limitations and by the pain which has so encumbered her in the past. She has carried on the work here on the Earth plane for the last 50 years because that's where the work was needed...rest assured that her work now in the higher realms will simply be an extension of that work.

www.ingramcontent.com/pod-product-compliance
Lightning Source LLC
LaVergne TN
LVHW051516070426
835507LV00023B/3142